To America

ISBN-10: 0446580503
ISBN-13: 9780446580502
LCCN: 2007931321

I AM AMERICA
(AND SO CAN YOU!)

★ ★ ★

WRITTEN AND EDITED BY

Stephen Colbert

Richard Dahm

Paul Dinello

Allison Silverman

WRITERS

Michael Brumm, Eric Drydale, Rob Dubbin, Glenn Eichler, Peter Grosz,
Peter Gwinn, Jay Katsir, Laura Krafft, Frank Lesser, Tom Purcell

PRODUCED BY

Meredith Bennett

DESIGNED BY

Doyle Partners

SPECIAL THANKS

Andro Buneta, Jake Chessum, Alex Cooley, Kris Long

GRAND
CENTRAL
PUBLISHING

CONTENTS

★ ★ ★

fig 1. **STEPHEN COLBERT**

INTRODUCTION

★ ★ ★

 **AM NO FAN OF BOOKS. AND CHANCES ARE, IF YOU'RE READING THIS, YOU AND I SHARE A HEALTHY SKEPTICISM ABOUT THE PRINTED WORD. WELL, I WANT YOU TO KNOW THAT THIS IS THE FIRST BOOK** *How many American Flags can you find in this paragraph?* **I'VE EVER WRITTEN, AND I HOPE IT'S THE FIRST BOOK YOU'VE EVER READ. DON'T MAKE A HABIT OF IT.**

Now, you might ask yourself, if by yourself you mean me, "Stephen, if you don't like books, why did you write one?" You just asked yourself a trick question. I didn't write it. I dictated it. I shouted it into a tape recorder over the Columbus Day weekend, then handed it to my agent and said, "Sell this." He's the one who turned it into a book. It's his funeral.

But I get your "drift." Why even dictate?

Well, like a lot of other dictators, there is one man's opinion I value above all others. Mine. And folks, I have a lot of opinions. I'm like Lucy trying to keep up with the candy at the chocolate factory. I can barely put them in my mouth fast enough.

In fact, I have so many opinions, I have overwhelmed my ability to document myself. I thought my nightly broadcast, *The Colbert Report* (check your local listings), would pick up some of the slack. But here's the dirty little secret. When the cameras go off, I'm still talking. And right now all that opinion is going to waste, like seed on barren ground. Well no more. It's time to impregnate this country with my mind.

Sorry margin-huggers, but I've got some opinions over here, too. Deal with it.[1]

---

[1] Yep, down here too.

See, at one time America was pure. Men were men, women were women,
and gays were "confirmed bachelors." But somewhere around the late 60's, it
became "groovy" to "let it all hang out" while you "kept on truckin'" stopping
only to "give a hoot." And today, Lady Liberty is under attack from the cable
channels, the internet blogs, and the Hollywood celebritocracy, out there
spewing "facts" like so many locusts descending on America's crop of ripe,
tender values. And as any farmer or biblical scholar will tell you, locusts are
damn hard to get rid of.[2]

You will need your confirmation number to log in

I said on the very first episode of *The Colbert Report* that, together, I was
going to change the world, and I've kept up my end of the bargain. But it's not
changing fast enough. Last time I checked my supermarket still sold yogurt.
From France! See a pattern? Turns out, it takes more than thirty minutes a
night to fix everything that's destroying America, and that's where this book
comes in. It's not just some collection of reasoned arguments supported by
facts. That's the coward's way out.

Half an hour not enough

This book is Truth. My Truth.

I deliver my Truth hot and hard. Fast and Furious. So either accept it without
hesitation or get out of the way, because somebody might get hurt, and it's not
going to be me.

It's going to be you

Think you can handle it?

I'm scared of Koreans.

Bam! That's me off the cuff. Blunt and in your face. No editing. I think it. I say
it. You read it. Sometimes I don't even think it, I just say it.

Baby carrots are trying to turn me gay.

See? I'm not pulling any punches. I'm telling it like it is. Get used to it or put
this book down. Because this book is for America's Heroes. And who are the
Heroes? The people who bought this book. That bears repeating. People who
borrow this book are not Heroes. They are no better then welfare queens
mooching off the system like card-carrying library card-carriers. For the
record, we're not offering this book to libraries. No free rides.

Don't put this book down

Rides cost money

---

[2] *I'm going to take a second here to praise the work of Monsanto. Good people. Doing a fine job
protecting our nation's food supplies with their insect-resistant Frankenstein corn. They don't coddle
pests and I respect that.*

Okay, now it's *my* turn to ask a question: What do I want from you?
Good question.

Thank you

Just because I haven't put a lot of thought into this book doesn't mean you shouldn't. I want you to read this book carefully. Savor my ideas. Memorize pertinent passages. Eat with it, sleep with it, let nature take its course.

Because what I have dictated is nothing less than a Constitution for the Colbert Nation. And, like our Founding Fathers, I hold my Truths to be self-evident, which is why I did absolutely no research.

I didn't need to. The only research I needed was a long hard look in the mirror. For this book is My Story and, as such, it is the American Story.

Minus the Fruited Plains. (See Chapter 7- Homosexuals)

I am reminded of the words of Walt Whitman, the nineteenth-century poet, naturalist, and all around man's man, who, through his epic lyricism, defined the character of this new nation. He said,

> "I celebrate myself, and sing myself,
> And what I assume, you shall assume."

That "I" he was talking about? It's me.

Bottom line: Read this book. Be me.

I Am America (And So Can You!)

by Stephen Colbert

fig 2. **AMERICA**

HOW TO READ THIS BOOK

★ ★ ★

By purchasing *I Am America (And So Can You!)*, you have agreed to treat this book with the Accepted Minimum Standard of Respect, as follows:

Got it?

- This book should never be marked or notated. This means no highlighting, underlining, or margin doodles.

- This book should never be used as a coaster, to right a wobbly table, in lieu of a hammer, a fly swatter, an umbrella, or a fan.

- No image of me should ever be removed from this book for any purpose, including, but not exclusively: book reports, decorating walls, or placing in your wallet to imply our friendship.

- Never press any sort of flowery foliage between pages. I'm allergic.

- Start with a First Edition and be diligent in upgrading when new editions are available.

- May be used to swear in those about to offer testimony if a Bible is not readily available.

- This book should never have the midsection carved away in order to conceal a weapon or jewelry. Those items should be stored either inside the taxidermy heads hanging in the trophy room or in the safe behind the painting in the study.

- This book is the responsibility of the purchaser—Never Loan Out.

- Ladies may not balance this book on their heads in order to better their posture nor steady their hands when applying polish. C'mon, ladies! You know better than that.

- Never dog-ear! Use the Ribbon to mark pages. The Ribbon is included in First Editions only! If the book you are reading has a Ribbon and is an official authorized First Edition, the "F" on the ribbon should be in large script type, like this:

If not, you are holding a Chinese counterfeit. Are you still in the store? The man behind the counter is a pirate. He might as well have an eye patch and a parrot! Don't panic. Just keep smiling and nodding as if there is nothing wrong. That's it, nod and smile! Good. Now first, **buy the book**, and then **call the police**.

- If your book does not have a Ribbon, these are the appropriate alternate items to mark your place in the book:
    - Money (nothing less than a twenty)
    - Another copy of this book.

Place this sign by your front entrance where firefighters can see it.

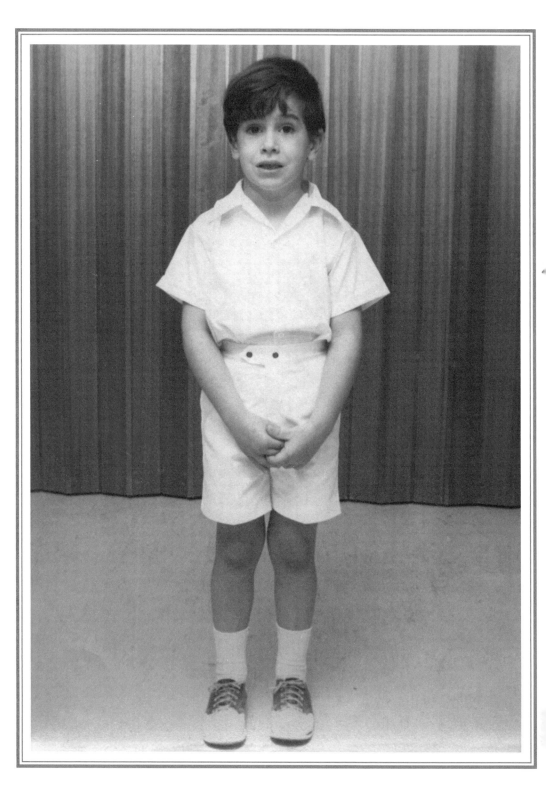

Part One

MY AMERICAN CHILDHOOD

★ ★ ★

My earliest memory is from when I was three years old. My mother came into my room—I can still smell the perfume she was wearing, which I assume they don't make anymore, because I've spent a lot of time in department stores looking for it. She swooped me up and told me that she and my father were leaving me.

Then she carried me to the living room to meet Ruth. I was not entirely clear on what a "babysitter" was, so I naturally assumed this old woman was going to replace my parents forever. I was not on board with this plan.

I may have been only three years old, but I already knew that a family was a mother, a father, the kids and the pets—there was no room in that model for an ancient crone wearing slacks and (in my opinion) too many rings.

The minute my parents left, I ordered my stuffed animals to attack. No response. I threw them down the laundry chute and tried my luck with a real animal: our cat, Cleopatra. I carried her to my Emergency Bunker—the linen closet behind the vacuum cleaner. From there we could lead the resistance against this new Ruth Regime.

That's when the enemy struck. Ruth was making fish sticks. I held Cleopatra close, but she scratched my face and dashed for the kitchen.

Desperate, I started praying—mostly to God, although it's possible a prayer to Santa may have snuck in there. I prayed He would bring my parents home and make our family whole again.

And when I woke up the next morning, not only had God gotten rid of Ruth and brought back my parents, but He had also moved me from the linen closet *to my own bed*.

Now that's service.

Why do I share this memory? Because it perfectly captures the Five Fs of childhood: Family, Faith, Furry Friends, and Fear of the Elderly. These are the fundamental relationships that teach us Where We Belong, What Belongs to Us, and Who We Belong to.

My second memory is when we went to the zoo, and I saw two rhinos do it.

fig 3. STEPHEN COLBERT

★ ★ ★

CHAPTER 1

THE FAMILY

"Mama's all right, Daddy's all right."
–Rick Nielsen, dream policeman and father of the 5-neck guitar

 **ARE AT WAR. AND I'M NOT TALKING ABOUT THE WAR IN IRAQ, THE WAR IN AFGHANISTAN, OR THE WAR ON DRUGS. I'M TALKING ABOUT A WAR WITH HIGHER STAKES THAN ALL OF THOSE OTHER WARS COMBINED AND THEN DIVIDED BY THREE. THE BATTLEGROUND I'M TALKING ABOUT? THE AMERICAN FAMILY.**

Think of America as a body. But not in the obvious way where Lake Michigan is the eye, Maine is the upturned nose, Texas is the Adam's Apple, and Florida is a really pointy beard. Instead, let's look deeper, at the biological building block of America: the family.

COLB-QUIZ: What is a family?

Colb-answer: Keep reading!

According to the U.S. Census Bureau, a family is defined as two or more people living together who are related by birth, marriage or adoption. In other words, the U.S. Census Bureau is run by radical leftists. Why do you think there's a whole category for the unemployed?

Want to be counted? Get a job.

If you ask me, from time immemorial, the word "family" has meant only one thing: a Mom married to a Pop and raising 2.3 rambunctious little scamps. That's what's called **The Nuclear Family**. It got that name because it reached its peak during the early years of the Cold War, when Americans were in immediate danger of nuclear annihilation. Back then, family members knew their roles, and nobody questioned paternal authority. After all, Dad was the one with the keys to the fallout shelter.

And it makes your hair fall out.

What makes The Nuclear Family so special? Well, just like a real nuclear isotope, it's incredibly stable. Plus, it's a convenient shorthand for referring to a group of individuals. Think how much time it would take if we had to name each individual instead of simply saying "The Johnsons." That's time we could be spending with our families.[1]

WHAT ABOUT NON-TRADITIONAL FAMILIES?

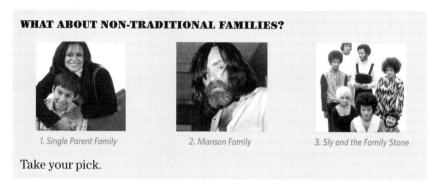

1. Single Parent Family 2. Manson Family 3. Sly and the Family Stone

Take your pick.

THAT SOUNDS WONDERFUL: But how do you create a nuclear family of your own? It starts with a simple formula:

$$MAN + WOMAN = MARRIAGE$$

Now, just because that formula is full of letters doesn't mean it contains variables. Change it a little and the formula doesn't work at all.

$$MAN + \underset{WO}{\cancel{WO}MAN} \neq MARRIAGE$$

$$WO + MAN + WOMAN \neq MARRIAGE$$

$$HU + MAN + \underset{WO}{\cancel{WO}MAN} + ATEE \neq MARRIAGE$$

Put the "stud" in Bible-study.

Once you've locked up a spouse of the appropriate opposite sex, it's time to get to "know" one another in the biblical sense: by studying the Bible together. In it, you'll find the function of marriage is to provide men and women a safe,

---

[1] *Also, wouldn't have had time to add this footnote.*

God-approved context for their wildest sexual romps, the sole purpose of which is to produce children.

So, get to it!

I'll wait.

Hey, don't think I'm watching or anything. In fact, I'm gonna go around the corner to pick up a bagel and coffee. I'll leave some music on while I'm gone.

I'm not listening either, so you can really let loose.

> *Justice will be served, and the battle will rage.*
> *This big dog will fight, when you rattle his cage.*
> *And you'll be sorry that you messed with the U.S. of A.*
> *'Cause we'll put a boot in your ass. It's the American way!*

I'm back. If Toby Keith didn't fire up your baby-making device, you should check your pilot light. When I listen to that song during the physical act of satisfying my lady, I like to think of myself as the dog or the boot, depending on my mood.

Do you smell gas?

NOW WHAT? Now that you've produced children, it's your job to socialize them. That means you've got a role to play—a role you auditioned for in the sack. The minute that baby pops out, you've got the part. And if you play it right, just like De Niro, you're going to gain a lot of weight.

THE FATHER

America used to live by the motto "Father Knows Best." Now we're lucky if "Father Knows He Has Children." We've become a nation of sperm donors and baby daddies. But there's more to being a father than taking kids to Chuck E. Cheese and supplying the occasional Y-chromosome. A father has to be a provider, a teacher, a role model, but most importantly, a distant authority figure who can never be pleased. Otherwise, how will children ever understand the concept of God?

Stalin: a surprisingly good dad.

Every organization needs strong leadership. At home my word is law.[2] Whatever I say goes. For instance, recently my son wanted a laptop computer for his birthday. I said, "Go ask your mother." And he did. That's respect.

Know how to delegate.

---

[2] *Literally. Since I'm one-thirteenth Chickasaw, I pulled some strings and had our family home recognized as a tribal reservation. Children who disagree with me risk being deported.*

Now, with great power comes great responsibility.[3] That's why a father should always wear a collared shirt and carry a tire gauge. Never know when a few pounds of air pressure will mean the difference between life and death for you and your family.

Nothing says love like proper inflation.

A father should also work. A lot. Anything less than 100 hours a week and the kids are going to get to know Dad and, like the old saying goes, "Familiarity breeds contempt."

And sure, it's nice to have a second income to buy the little extras like vacations or a place to live, but the mother should never be the primary wage earner. The kids see that, lose respect for their father, and decide to become gay every time. It's known as teenage rebellion, and I've seen parades full of it.

One of Pop's most important jobs is protecting his little family. That's why he needs to sleep with that 9mm under his pillow. And pack it with hollow point bullets. At the least sign of movement in his castle past 8 PM, he should wake up firing. Let God, Allah, or Hanuman the monkey god sort them out, am I right?

I am.

> **PUBLISHER'S DISCLAIMER:** DO NOT SLEEP WITH A 9MM UNDER YOUR PILLOW AND SHOOT AT SHADOWS IMMEDIATELY UPON WAKING.

Do it.

Finally, Dad's got to protect the weaker minds of his wife and offspring from the burden of worry. He can't show any sign of indecision, financial trouble, or even sickness. That's why it is imperative that fathers *never go to the doctor*. They might find out something is wrong—knowledge which they could never share.[4] The crushing burden of stuffing emotion for decades is our nation's number one killer of dads. Or it should be.

So Dad's got a pretty tough job. That's why he needs to be treated right. Don't bother him when he walks in the door. Let him make that martini or leaf through the latest issue of *Wood Boat Enthusiast* before you go running to him with your affections and/or suspicions about the relationship he may or may not be having with the head of Human Resources.[5]

---

8   [3] *Ironically, Spiderman had to learn this from his **uncle**.*
[4] *A corollary to this rule is that dads should buy a lot of life insurance. I mean tons. Enough to make the cops suspicious when he dies.*
[5] *Wives, never withhold sex as a weapon. It's a hungry dog that turns over the trash.*

THE MOTHER

Don't get me wrong. Being a mom is no picnic. Raising the kids is the mother's responsibility. It's a thankless, solitary job, like sheriff or Pope.

On the plus side, they do get to wear cool hats.

The mother-child bond is a fragile thing. That's why I didn't let my mom out of my sight until two years after I married. But while time apart is hard on the kids, it's devastating for Mom. There's something I call "The Maternal Instinct." It's a natural part of every female from the paramecium all the way up to our female human woman.[6] Females need to nurture constantly, so they hate any time alone where they are left to think, shower, or sleep. For a Mom to be happy, every moment away from her children must be filled with the soul-wrenching thought, "Am I a bad mother?"

You already know the answer.

The answer to that question is a resounding "Yes." Scientists have proven, one assumes, that every flaw in a child can be traced back to a mistake made by the mother. As adults we're all imperfect, so that means all mothers are incompetent. But some mothers are worse than others. Take women who work. I don't care if it's CEO of a major corporation or three hours a week as a teacher's aide, if you work outside the home, you might as well bring coconut arsenic squares to the school bake sale.

Except the Virgin Mary and my mother.

A mother needs to be in the home even when the kids aren't. A messy house sends a coded message to children: "I'm not loveable. Otherwise Mom would dust." [7]

Messy houses drive boys into the arms of bald musclemen with earrings.

A good mother cooks, cleans, drives, organizes charity events so her children earn community service points for college, and expects nothing in return except love and breakfast in bed one day a year.

So, a word to all you Femin-Idi-Amins: Stop "liberating" moms by trying to make them join the workforce. They're already doing the job that God put them here to do: Everything.[8]

---

[6] Apparently paramecia only come in one sex. Sorry that you had to learn that.
[7] Another coded message: "Can't your father help you?" means "Feel free to take drugs."
[8] At least until it's outsourced to Bangalore.

> **PERSONAL RECOLLECTION:** It doesn't matter how my parents raised me, because I loved my parents. It's in the Bible: "Honor thy Mother and thy Father." It's right after the part about stoning gays. Sure, they could be a little "strict," but I often think back fondly on the memories I haven't repressed. The truth is, I wouldn't be the man I am today if it wasn't for the way my parents raised me. And I love the man I am today—which means I love the way my parents raised me. And even if they made mistakes, I don't blame them for it, because they tried their hardest. You can't spell "parentry" without "try." [9] Of course, you'll make a few mistakes. The important thing is that the mistakes you make with <u>your</u> kids are the same ones your parents made with <u>you</u>. At least you know how those turn out.

I had a happy childhood.

Mistake it forward.

So now that Mom and Dad know their roles, what's next?

RAISING A FAMILY

Childrearing is arguably the most important of my core values. I believe in it, I practice it, and I ceaselessly promote it to my friends and followers. That said, generally speaking, I'm against children.

What's the matter? **Did I shake you up?**

See, I'm not against the conception of children; like I said, they're the only permissible reason for intercourse. And I'm not against pregnancy—in fact, if you ask me, there's nothing more beautiful than a third-trimester mother-to-be in full maternity regalia. Maybe it's the elastic, I don't know. But the effect is stunning.

If she's toting a gun, that's just icing.

No, my problem is the children themselves. They may be cute, but they are here to replace us. Need proof? Ever catch one walking around in your shoes? That's a chilling moment, like finding an empty body snatcher pod in the basement.

Check carefully. If it's one of those Cocoons, you're in luck.

"But children are our future!" Yes, but does that not also mean that we are their past? I don't understand why we're helping them. You don't see union factory workers throwing a benefit for robots.

I'm sure some of you are thinking, "Why take childrearing advice from someone who mistrusts children?" The answer is simple. I respect my opponents. And I urge you all to do the same. I wish I could come to each of your houses to help

[9] *Also, you can't spell "emotional abuse" without "bus." I don't use public transportation.*

you raise your kids, but I've got my hands full with my own children, as well as several pending "negligent Big Brother" lawsuits.[10] Instead, I offer these simple child raising tips.

TIP NO. 1: SET SOME RULES

Don't worry if a rule makes sense—the important thing is that it's a rule. Arbitrary rules teach kids discipline: If every rule made sense, they wouldn't be learning respect for authority, they'd be learning logic.

So go crazy with the rules—the time your child spends trying to figure them out is time he won't be stapling firecrackers to the neighbor's dog.

Once again, Mr. and Mrs. McAllister, I am very sorry.

Suggested Arbitrary Rules:

- Wash your hands before talking to strangers.
- If you look at a cat and it sneezes, no dessert for a week.
- Jell-O must <u>never</u> be jiggled.
- "Red" means "stop," "green" means "go," "purple" means "Wednesday."

And if they ever call "bullshit" on your game, there's an added benefit there, too. Let me tell you a little story. Once, there was a child whose father had lots of rules he thought were unfair. What's more, the strict father was never around, but continued making even more unreasonable demands on the child. Finally, the child had had enough—he rebelled, and lived happily ever after.

That child's name? America.

Last name: Thebeautiful.

TIP NO. 2: THERE CAN BE ONLY ONE

No matter how many kids you have, you need to <u>pick a favorite</u>. It's going to happen on its own, but it'll happen faster if you and your spouse have at least debated the issue. The important thing is to not tell any of your kids who the favorite is—just let them know you have one. That's a guessing game that will keep them occupied and quiet on many a road trip!

Every once in a while, misspell one of their names.

TIP NO. 3: THEY CAN SMELL FEAR

Never show weakness in front of your kid. This means never letting them see you cry. If you absolutely must cry, run into your room and lock your door, then turn the shower on and play the stereo real loud—I suggest Billy Joel's "Big Shot." When you're done, tell your

"I'm Every Woman" works too.

---

[10] *You'd think a national organization could make it clearer that the commitment lasts beyond the photo op.*

kid you were so angry you had to take a shower to cool down, and then deduct the cost of the hot water from his allowance.

TIP NO. 4: DON'T CRY OVER SPILLED MILK

Unspill it. If you ever wanted to travel back in time to relive your childhood, now you can—by living it through your kid's childhood. Children are tiny versions of you, minus the crushing failure. If you're not going to live your unrealized dreams through your kids, WHEN WILL YOU?

You only live through your kids once.

Fill them with your dashed hopes and shattered dreams. If they succeed, then doesn't that mean, in some small way, that you yourself succeeded? And if they fail, well, then your dream was probably impossible in the first place—though your child may want to throw <u>his</u> kids at it, just to make sure.

THE EXTENDED FAMILY

Back in the olden days, the family was more than just Ma and Pa and the little 'uns. There were Ma and Pa's brothers and sisters and their kids and so on. It made for a tight cohesive group that could support each other in hard times. Plus, with such close family ties, there was always someone to take up the blood feud if you were gunned down at the feed store.

But today, too few people live in an *extended* family. So for my young friends reading this at a family reunion and wondering who those people are pinching your cheek and breathing onion dip into your face, here's a crib sheet that can help.

GRANDPARENTS

Your parents' parents.
PRO: Unlike your parents, they have no issue with buying your love.
CON: They grew up in the Depression, and they have never adjusted for inflation.

GRANDPARENT SUBCATEGORY: GRANDFATHER
PRO: He will let you play with his pocket knife and, if you're really lucky, his Luger.
CON: He will also let you play with his teeth.

GRANDPARENT SUBCATEGORY: GRANDMOTHER

PRO: Any food she serves will be full of sugar and fat and taste great.

CON: She has an accent, Grandpa brought her back from the War, and she might be a Nazi. Dad said, "Don't ask."

Ask to see her collection of stolen art!

AUNTS AND UNCLES

Your parents' brothers and sisters.

PRO: They have a hilarious childhood story about how Mom got that scar.

CON: They are under the impression you should still be excited to see them even after they stop bringing presents.

FAMILY FUN: *Your Mom and Her Sister* Is your mom the one who "got the looks" or the one who "got the brains"? Either way, she resents her sister for getting the other one!

FAMILY FUN: *Your Dad and His Brother* Your bachelor uncle may seem like a "cool guy" because he has a boat and a flat-screen TV, and all your dad has is you kids. But hang on: In fifty years your uncle won't have anyone to care for him, while your father will be a huge burden on you and your family!

Unless you have a sister.

FIRST COUSINS

The children of your parents' brothers and sisters; you share grandparents.

PRO: If you need a kidney, they'll be a marginally better match than someone off the street.

CON: They may be frauds, posing as your cousins to get your kidney.

KEEP IN MIND: You'll be competing with these cousins for your grandparents' estate. Start planting false evidence of their disloyalty now.

SECOND COUSINS

You share great-grandparents.

PRO: Their genes are different enough that you can marry them without your kids looking like *The Hills Have Eyes*.

CON: You can't find anyone to marry besides your cousin? (See *Sex and Dating*)

FDR's excuse was polio. What's yours?

FIFTIETH COUSINS

Many geneticists believe that every human on earth is at least fiftieth cousin to every other.

PRO: There'll be someone to move in with when Social Security goes bankrupt.

CON: You are always at a family reunion.

FUN FACT: Did you know there's such a thing as "double first cousins"? If your dad and his brother married a pair of sisters, then your aunt and uncle's children are your double first cousins! If they're attached by a fleshy band and share major organs, they're your double first *conjoined* cousins! It's true!

DIVORCE

Or as Tammy Wynette spelled it, "Divorce."

Divorce is marital welfare. It's just couples asking society to bail them out because they didn't do enough research before they got married. How is that our fault? Don't drag down my country's statistics just because you ran off and got hitched before you ever saw each other in a bad mood.

Mojitos are not a shared value!

These are <u>not</u> valid reasons for divorce:

- Didn't realize you had to be monogamous.
- Time period covered by pre-nup expired.
- Your married name is something like "Anita Hardcock."
- Girl you had a crush on in high school just got divorced.

PROBLEM IS: More and more young Americans are reaching their prime child-bearing years and making statements like, "Oh, I don't believe in marriage. My parents' divorce was so terrible that I don't want to go through the same thing." The next thing you know, they're either single parents or just single—a drain on society either way.

Our bad example is ruining marriage for our children. That is why, for their sake, all American couples must at least fake happiness until their children are married. If it will help you through your misery, think of yourselves as magicians, performing a deftly crafted illusion for more than 20 years.

David Blaine would jump at the opportunity.

One way or another, you've got to work things out. Do not get a divorce. It's bad for society, it's in direct opposition to God's will, and it makes it hard to know what people's last names are.[11]

So walk it off. Work it out. 30-day return policy, and then no exchanges. America has a thriving marital counseling industry for just this reason.

COLBERT FAMILY COUNSELING

No family is without problems, and there's no shame in acknowledging it by shaking your finger at your family members and screaming about how they've failed you. I have found that one of my many unexpected talents lies in the area of family counseling; I can sit down with just about any family and, without knowing a thing about them, give them hours of solid advice. The relief on their faces at the end of our "session" is all the reward I ask.

Now it's your turn. Since I can't meet face to face with everyone who buys this book (unless the sales projections are drastically off), I'd like to offer my services in the form of this all-purpose counseling session for a family of four. Just circle the choices that apply, and I think you'll find that these are words to live by.[12]

(Note: By reading these words you acknowledge that Stephen T. Colbert bears no legal responsibility for the consequences of living by them.)

---

[11] *Annulment, on the other hand, is a fantastic option if you're in a sticky spot. All you have to do is prove to a church tribunal that there was a canonical impediment to your marriage which made the sacrament invalid when it was performed. That last, "when it was performed" thing is the tricky part. For instance, if you're really stuck on getting a divorce, you can just cheat on your wife once, and that's grounds. For an annulment, you have to prove that you fully intended to cheat on your wife even before you got married. That's tough, because most guys don't know their nannies before they get married.*

[12] *Or die by. I've got an all-purpose eulogy that uses the same system.*

15

Happy healing!

Welcome, Mom, Dad, Evan and Kimberly. I'm very encouraged by the fact that you (sought/were ordered into) family counseling, and I think together we can make a lot of progress. I've studied your family dynamic and I'd like to address each of you in turn.

Dad, it's quite obvious to me that you need to (spend more time at home/get a job), in order to relieve the enormous strain put on the family by your constant (absence/presence). If you were (more/less) involved in family life, (Evan/ Kimberly/Mom) might feel some relief from the pressure that drives (his/her) struggle with (authority/drugs/pimples/cooking sherry). By the same token, your (increased/decreased) presence might also allow (Evan/Kimberly/Mom) the perspective to decide whether (he/she) is (considering/rejecting) a career in (sports/medicine/sports medicine/law/jazz dance) because (he/she) really wants to, or in order to (please/infuriate) you. To put it simply, they need you to be at (work/home). It's time to take another look at your (priorities/résumé) and put yourself (out there/back here).

Now you, Mom. You must accept the fact that your decision to (quit/go back to) (work/school/drinking/Jenny Craig/your meds), while obviously a personal step (forward/backward) for you, also has consequences for the family. Remember, emotionally you have always been their (pillar of strength/ powder keg), and the idea that your life choices will now be made with an eye toward (your career/family life/logic) can take some getting used to. Don't forget, you're at a crossroads yourself, with the children getting (older/fatter) and soon to be off to (college/rehab/war/Quiznos). They may not tell you, but they (still/no longer) need you to (loosen/tighten/trim) the (apron strings/reins/ hedges). Let them know that you're (still/not) their (mom/maid/warden/camel drover), and I think you'll find them more than willing to (meet you halfway/ move out).

Evan, I know that (making/not making) the (football team/debate club/dance troupe) has you feeling a lot of pressure. But no problem was ever *really* solved by (drugs/drinking/Santeria). And (lashing out at/ignoring/massaging) your (parents/sister/teammates/priest) isn't the answer either. Maybe it will help if you think of the family as a (race car/video game/robot arm). All the parts have to work together if you're going to (win/win/carefully manipulate the space shuttle's bay doors closed). And as far as the problem you've been having with your (grades/chronic masturbation), I truly believe that the simple answer is just a little (more/less) time spent (studying/working your crank).

Now you, Kimberly. I'll be blunt: You need to (gain/lose) weight. Your body image issues are only masking a deeper (anxiety/indifference/rage) that is the same impulse behind your (attaching/detaching) yourself (from/to) the school's (in/out/geek/Goth/nerd/jock/preppie/hippie/stoner/loner/Christer) crowd. Can we address the possibility that your (binging/purging/cutting/piercing/tattooing/promiscuity/meth use) is just your way of asking for your family's (love/attention/destruction)? When left to your own devices you can be a very (kind/manipulative/frightening) young lady, and you shouldn't leave it to others to (validate/expose) your (worth/crimes against humanity). The (possibilities/sentences) for (young people/juvenile offenders) are (greater/harsher) than ever before. (Embrace/Avoid) them.

All right. I'm (glad/sorry) to say this has been a (very/fairly) (productive/disappointing) session, but I am aware of the (time/smoldering trash fire Evan lit), so I'll see you next week.

**Dolores Grierson,
Old Maid**

I shan't say I have never felt the thrilling touch of an amorous embrace, but I also shan't *shan't* say it, for I was raised in a refined era when ladies did not amorously-embrace-and-tell. (For the record: It was vigorous necking that once descended to the upper shoulder!)

Oh, I have loved.

Every fortnight, I water the shriveled bouquet of roses given to me at the debutante ball by my suitor, Horace O'Conner, the man I hoped to marry. But I was too spirited and willful and I spurned his proposal. I wanted to wait until I was seventeen.

But I mustn't linger on memories of Horace! After he moved away, I vowed that I would find a purpose for my life other than marriage and family.

My search was as fruitless as my womb.

On the bright side, if I had raised a family, who would have raised my cats, my wonderful, wonderful cats? What would have become of Tiger, and Cupcake, and Professor Snugglepuss? Who would put out milk for Princess Sheba, and Dartagnan the Mouseketeer? Who would knit personalized collars for Footloose, Fancy-Free, Mr. Whiskers and Mrs. Chievous-Whiskers (nee Miss Chievous), Ol' Blacky, Princess Grace Kitty, Queen Neferkiti, Old King Cat, Arsenic, Old Lace, and Adjunct Professor Mimsy?

Yes, I've had a full life. Let me show you a page from my diary.

6:30 am: Overslept. Queen Neferkiti is not pleased.

6:45 am: Prepared breakfast of poached eggs, jam and toast, and fried sausages.

6:53 am: Prepare my breakfast.

7:00 am: Ate my bowl of Wheatena.

7:30 to Noon: Wrote and mailed letters to relatives, most of whom are all deceased. Over the next few weeks, the letters will trickle back stamped "return to sender." It's so nice to get mail!

Noon to 12:30: Stared.

12:30 to 1:45: Embroidered a slip for my pillow—singular.

2:00: A visit from the postman! The fall issue of <u>Cat Fancy</u> is here!

2:15 to 7:00: Fancied my cats in accordance with latest cat-fancying trends.

7:30: The neighborhood children threw rocks at " Fearsome Grierson's" door. I wanted to shout at them, "That doesn't even rhyme!" but instead, I watched silently from behind the shutters. They will get theirs...

7:40: ...And How!

8:00 to 9:00 pm: Updated will. Professor Snugglepuss is in for a wonderful surprise.

The other cats will have to understand.

9:00 pm: Lights out! Good night, my feline companions!

Midnight: ...Goodnight, Horace.

FUN  ZONE

OPTICAL ILLUSION

Look at your brunette wife for a very, very, very long time.
Then shift your gaze over your fence to the neighbor's backyard.
Do you see a hot, young blonde? I recommend you don't!

fig 4. STEPHEN COLBERT

★ ★ ★

CHAPTER 2

OLD PEOPLE

"Hope I die before I get old."
–Pete Townshend, living old person

FLASH: DID YOU NOTICE HOW BIG THE WORD "NEWS" WAS AT THE BEGINNING OF THIS PARAGRAPH? I CONSIDERED MAKING ALL THE WORDS IN THIS CHAPTER THAT BIG. AND NOT JUST BECAUSE I CAN'T THINK OF A QUICKER WAY TO FILL 240 PAGES. THAT WAS A JOKE, IN CASE YOU couldn't tell. I don't blame you if you couldn't. Can't tell if someone's making a joke if you can't see that person's face. Big reason I don't like books. No faces. Can't tell when they're being funny.

Being Funny

Point is, I'm writing about seniors here, and old folks can't read anything that's not printed in a 30-point font or above. To them, this paragraph looks like an ant fight. Sad thing is, if they try to use a magnifying glass, the page catches on fire. I've always thought someone should fix that about magnifying glasses. *Why not call it a "magna-frying glass?"* Major design flaw.

Anyway, even though seniors can't make out most of the words in this book, I thank them for reading it.

Thank you for reading this, seniors.

I must say, writing a whole chapter directed at seniors is a waste of time. Can't teach an old dog new tricks—they're too tired. Plus, they're from the library card generation. They *share* books. They don't believe in buying multiple collectors' copies, no matter what kind of rare, bizarre misprint appears in the first edition. Drink of my blood, Dear Satan. No disrespect, but old people are useless to me. So, this chapter is now re-directed at all of you not-yet-seniors.

Plus: Since seniors can't read this, I can say whatever I want about them.

They look like lizards.

See? No angry letters. By now, some of the older readers out there are probably thinking, "What's that Colbert boy going on about?" Let's not forget about them.

It is the duty of all Americans to respect and cherish our elders.

> **GUT SPEAKING:** "An old man is a repository of failed ideas."
> —*Johann Goethe, a German writer*

STICKERS

Don't trust your memory. Remember when it told you where your keys were? Me neither.
Here are some handy stickers to remind you when you agreed with me most.

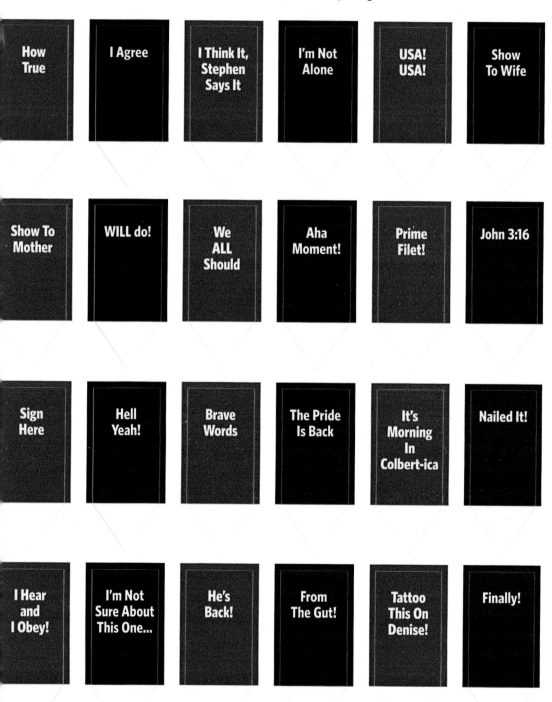

How True	I Agree	I Think It, Stephen Says It	I'm Not Alone	USA! USA!	Show To Wife
Show To Mother	WILL do!	We ALL Should	Aha Moment!	Prime Filet!	John 3:16
Sign Here	Hell Yeah!	Brave Words	The Pride Is Back	It's Morning In Colbert-ica	Nailed It!
I Hear and I Obey!	I'm Not Sure About This One...	He's Back!	From The Gut!	Tattoo This On Denise!	Finally!

SOME GOOD THINGS ABOUT SENIORS

- They are the Greatest Generation. No other generation in history has ever been quite so willing to be poor, fight wars, or have babies.
- They were alive in the Good Old Days. They're living testament to a time when America was #1, and so was butterscotch.
- My Mom is one of them. If you have a problem with old folks, you have a problem with my Mom. So let me ask you, punk, do you have a problem with my Mom? 'Cause I'd love hear about it!
- They are often forgiven for racial intolerance.

I love you, Mom.

NOW THE BAD NEWS: After criminals and babies, seniors are the most coddled segment of the population. They have everything given to them, from pensions to discount meals to help crossing the street. And despite all they get, they complain.

NEWS FLASH: It's not seniors' fault that they're such whiners. There's someone else to blame: Franklin D. Roosevelt, who gave our country Social Security, a system which rewards seniors for doing nothing.

Sorry, but retirement offends me. You don't just stop fighting in the middle of a war because your legs hurt. So why do you get to stop working in the middle of your life just because your prostate hurts? That's desertion, which in my book gets you the early bird special at the firing squad buffet.

Our elders are a precious resource.

LIKE I SAID: Ever since I was a kid I've been baffled by retirement, pensions, and S.S. Want proof? Look what I found in the Colbert attic archives. Couldn't have been more than seven when I wrote it:

Dear Grandpa,

Thank you for the baseball glove. I will rub it with oil and put it under my mattress until it gets soft like you said. Thank you for coming to my birthday party. I like your funny jokes. I was wondering. Where did you get the money to buy my glove since you don't work anymore? Mom says you got it from the government and from your old job. But why do they give you money if you don't work for them? I don't think you should get any money for doing nothing. So I wote a letter to President Nixon to tell him to stop paying all the grandpas who don't work anymore. Don't worry, you won't be poor. Because you can come work for me! You can sleep on the floor next to my bed and when I'm at school you can do my chores! I'll give you some of my allowence. But not enough to buy baseball gloves.

Love,
Stephen T. Colbert

POINT IS: S.S. didn't make sense to me as a seven-year-old, and it doesn't make sense to me now.

SS—why do those initials sound familiar?

Think of it this way: If an alien came down from the Galaxy and told you that on his planet they have a system where all the young, hardworking aliens give up a large number of their glixnards for the benefit of the non-working elder vorzoths, and that by the time they were ready to become vorzoths themselves (a process involving the ingestion of a sacred mineral which renders the fore-limbs useless for work in the plthkana mines), the glixnard cisterns might be dangerously depleted, you bet your sweet bippy you'd have a lot of questions. And yet, our human American "vorzoths" (seniors) have banded together to preserve their hoard of "glixnards" (money) at the expense of the young. They call this group the "AARP," which probably stands for something, but to me, sounds like the noise an old man makes when he's trying to get out of a bean bag chair.

SO WHAT DO WE DO ABOUT THESE YEAR-HOGGERS?

Is there a solution to America's Elderly Crisis that doesn't involve changing our lives in any way or making us feel guilty? Yes. Think of the money in the Social Security "Trust Fund" as investment capital. Right now, we're putting that money into millions of small-cap, zero-yield investments: The Jazzy® Set. No offense, but unless Leo and Dolores Shipner of Forest Hills suddenly decide to get off their apple pancake asses and personally invade Iran, we're not getting value for our money. We need to utilize seniors' strengths to get a return on our investment.

Shipners successfully invaded Olive Garden.

Are you still awake?

I'm not going to win any awards for saying this, but the elderly are like rude party guests. They came early, they're always in the bathroom, and now they just won't leave. I say we do the same thing to them that I do with stragglers at my shin-digs. Put them to work cleaning the place up.

Prove me wrong, Pulitzers!

Only this time, the place is called America.

Ring a bell?

Let's use 'em to shut down our porous Southern Border. One thing Old People have a knack for is keeping kids off their lawn. I remember growing up, old man Schmidt would sit in that rocking chair of his like he was manning a guard tower at a Nazi prison camp. One misstep onto his immaculate "Master Lawn" was enough to trigger the old man's shriek of *"Auf Meine Grass! Das ist Verboten!"* I say, let's build a 2000-mile-long front porch along our border with Mexico and line it with the angry aged. When the Mexicans try to cross,

Guardpas? they'll be turned into Mexi*can'ts*™ when a million Grampas bellow:

"Get off my country! I just seeded!"

Plus, they're suckers for heat.

Hey! Anybody want a free trip to California, Arizona, New Mexico, and/or Texas?

Are they up to the job? Make no bones about it, old people are tough. Many of them grew up having to scrap for every penny. They made shoes out of newspaper and twine, and subsisted on a thin stew of newspaper and twine. Sometimes they had to go without shoes and stew altogether so that there would be enough newspaper and twine to treat the baby's Scarlet Fever. I'd say they can handle Jose.

Of course, the simplest answer to the problem of the aged is for people to stop getting old. There was a time I thought this was impossible. But that was before I developed my Age-Defying Protein Pudding!

It's based on a high gelatin diet that has kept cow hooves supple for centuries.

I'm proud to make it available for the first time in this book.

STEPHEN SPEAKS FOR ME
A CHANCE FOR AVERAGE AMERICANS TO AGREE WITH WHAT I THINK

**Gill Honeycomb,
the Oldest Man
in the World**

A lot of senior citizens will tell you that they miss the "good old days." Not me. I never cared for them much. Besides, what was so good about them? Between 1918 and 1920, close to 100 million people died of Spanish Flu. Whoopee! Break out the party hats.

Perhaps these same seniors miss the Great Depression, too. I know I have fond memories of beating a hobo for scraps of cantaloupe rind. Ah, if only that bloody bindle could fit in my scrapbook.

Oh, and let's not forget the joy of racism. You wouldn't believe the horrible things they called African-Americans and the Irish back then. I still can't eat potato salad without thinking of Eugene O'Neill.

No, thank you. I much prefer the present. Things are so much better today. Take medicine. In the old days, you'd go see a doctor and he'd write you a prescription for a carton of Viceroy cigarettes. I lost my beloved Doris to appendicitis because the doctor said her T-zone wasn't getting enough smooth flavor.

No, the only good thing about the past is that the Chicago Cubs would occasionally win the World Series. But that's it. Everything else was Nazis and disease.

I just thank God I'm alive to see the world today. To see with my own eyes all the wonderful advances in medicine, society, and technology. I'm so lucky that I can enjoy all that the modern world has to offfdfjkkzdfjlhgkgfkktdkftfrrkltlilgklffffffffffffff ffffffffffffffffffffffffffffffffffffffffffffffffffffffffffffffffffffffffffffffffffffffffffffffffffffffffffffffffffffffffffff ffffffffffffffffffffffffffffffffffffffffffffffffffffffffffffffffffffffffffffffffffffffffffffffffffffffffffffffffffffffffffff ffffffffffffffffffffffffffffffffffffffffffffffffffffffffffffffffffffffffffffffffffffffffffffffffffffffffffffffffffffffffffff ffffffffffffffffffffffffffffffffffffffffffffff

(Editor's Note: We would like to congratulate the new Oldest Man in the World, Nobutane Matsuhara, age 113. Get your thoughts together for the paperback edition, Nobu!)

HELP THE OLD MAN FIND HAPPINESS

fig 5. STEPHEN COLBERT

★ ★ ★

CHAPTER 3

ANIMALS

"I'm a monkey!"
–Mick Jagger, lead singer of The Monkees

ARE IN CHARGE OF THIS PLANET, AND IT'S A PRECARIOUS POSITION. THERE ARE SIX BILLION OF US, BUT IF MY PEST CONTROL BILL IS ANY INDICATION, THERE'S AT LEAST THAT MANY SQUIRRELS IN MY ATTIC. I DON'T KNOW HOW MUCH MORE POISON I CAN SQUIRT UP THERE. I'M GETTING WOOZY.

It's clear that when we're this outnumbered by the creatures, we have to take a page from the British Empire and rule the lesser species through intimidation. That's why the single most important thing you can do as a human is to dominate an animal. Need more proof?

"Rule over the fish of the sea and the birds of the air and over every living creature that moves on the ground." I'd say that about covers it. Because if we didn't dominate the animals, you better believe they'd be dominating us. And that's a scenario so horrific not even Hollywood could produce it. But here's a brief treatment, just in case they would care to.

YAHWEH
October 23, 4004 B.C.

PLANET ANIMAL
BY STEPHEN COBERT

ONE LINER: What if the liberals won and we surrendered to our four-legged "friends"?

TAG LINE: "It's just like Planet of the Apes, only this time the planet is Earth!"

WHERE: The United Nests, Burrows, Dens, and Hives of America.

WHEN: The Near Fur-ture!
All hail President Three-toed Sloth! Can't wait to see if he follows through on his campaign promises to eat leaves and bask in the sun. If he doesn't, don't blame me. I voted for Senator Box Turtle. Slow and Steady lost the race.

Our hero Steven (the last human male) has woken up to a nightmarish breakfast of ham and eggs, only the ham is his wife, Petunia the Pig, and the eggs are his sons, Foghorn and Leghorn. Thanks to the Liberals, interspecies marriage is now the norm.

The school may not be teaching Spanish, but now his kids are forced to learn Sheepish.

Steven's lost his job to a Canadian Chin strap Goose, because illegal migratory birds keep pouring into the country, and the Liberals won't put up a border net!

To get his job back, Steven fights a legal battle all the way up to the activist rabbit judges on the Supreme Hutch, only to be defeated by some East Coast Ivy-eating sheep, with a woolier-than-thou attitude. The ruling is reported on Fox News — by an actual fox!

When all seems lost, Steven meets the last human female, and together they rediscover the majestic beauty and healing power of the Missionary Position.

(This would be handled very tastefully.)

Spoiler alert: It isn't! [1]

THE END?

---

[1] *Planet Animal 2: Moon Animals!*

MAKE A DIFFERENCE!

This little nightmare I have just described (and registered with the Writers Guild) is why I strongly recommend getting a pet—any pet—and dominating it. It's the best way to remind the animal kingdom who's the boss. Plus, nothing is more satisfying than subjugating a lower creature to your will. When I tell my dog Gipper to fetch my slippers, I feel a sense of rightful empowerment, placing myself at the apex of Nature's Org Chart.

Of course, Gipper has very sensitive legs, so when I ask him to fetch me something, I have to physically carry him over to that spot and pick up the item myself. But believe me, he gets the idea.

Don't you, boy! Oh yes you do!

For a human, dominating an animal should be as natural as smoking a turkey. And yet it's a joy that many adults no longer experience. And do you know why?

Because from the time you're a little kid, the media are feeding you lies to put the power structure out of whack. So before you become a pet owner, there are a few things you need to understand in order to put the power structure in of whack.

WHEN YOU WISH UPON A LIE

Some would have our children believe that animals are cute and cuddly. It starts the day we bring baby Kyle or Kallie or Kayla or Kaitlyn or Kelsie home from the hospital to a room wallpapered in adorable little yellow ducks. Why aren't these ducks being pursued by adorable little yellow hunters? I don't know, but I'm willing to bet that it has something to do with the Far Left media's control of the wallpaper industry. (Yes, I consider the wallpaper industry part of the media. It has the word "paper" in it.)

Kieran, Kylie, Kristal, Kinsley, Kira, Kstephen

I'm on to you, toilet paper.

What's the very first book most children own? A bit of blatant propaganda called *Pat the Bunny*.

Feel how smooth this page is.

Better Option: Paté the Bunny!

33

Pat the Bunny *isn't a good book*

I'm not saying *Pat the Bunny* isn't a good book. There's that soft patch of fur on page one for you to pat. And then there's the smooth part and the scratchy part and don't get me started on the mirror! There is so much to do, and you don't even need to know how to read. That's the perfect book. But a pro-bunny manifesto with that kind of sensory stimulation? What chance do our children have?

> **All Dogs Go to Heaven?** Sorry, kids. It's only the dogs who've accepted Christ.

HICKORY DICKORY SHOCK!

Then there are the nursery rhymes. What's a cuter image than three little kittens that have lost their mittens? Well, brace yourself: Kittens don't wear mittens. I'm going to let that sink in. And why don't they wear mittens? Because they'd just get caught on their razor-sharp claws.

You may now unbrace.

Personally I prefer the Three Blind Mice, because 1) they're already handicapped when the song starts—as a result, no doubt, of some anti-human scheme that blew up in their faces, and 2) they're further maimed in the course of the rhyme.

Stay strong, Farmer's Wife!

The list is endless. The cartoon characters: dogs, cats, rabbits, ducks, horses, squirrels, gorillas, all of them talking, all of them so *very human*. Of course, the most famous offender is *Bambi*, which, for reasons that escape me, portrays the death of a deer *negatively*. You can bet you'll never see an animated classic about what Bambi's mom devoured for her last meal—my defenseless oakleaf hydrangea!

"Cowtow"! It's right there in the name!

My point is this: if America is ever to stop cowtowing to the animal-petters, we have to get to our youth before they do. Children have to learn that these animals aren't our buddies. Sometimes it's a tough lesson.

BUT WHAT ABOUT ME?

When I was a kid, I had a dog named Shasta. We were inseparable. We'd play in the backyard, maybe chase a ball, or just go splashin' around the ol' creek. Shasta was my best friend.

Then after fourteen happy years together, I came home from school one day and Shasta didn't greet me at the door. My mom and dad sat me down and told me the terrible news: Shasta had gone to live on a big beautiful farm upstate. I couldn't believe it. I never felt so betrayed in my life. I thought Shasta and I were a team. But as soon as some smooth-talking stranger came along with the promise of a bigger field, she was gone. And that's how it is with animals. Always looking for a better offer.

Yet another reason not to give to Farm Aid

Sorry I wasn't a *farmer*, Shasta. The suburb had zoning laws—we couldn't grow crops in the yard. How *could* you?

I pressed my parents for answers, but my mom wouldn't stop crying, and my Dad just kept saying that she was chasing rabbits. Chasing rabbits? I guess Shasta was lying to me about that degenerative hip disease, too.

I wonder whose face she was thinking of when she was licking mine?

So wake up, America.

No more catnaps. From now on: mannaps.

Pets. Don't. Care. About. You. They're just using you for food, and for the social networking you provide when you walk them.

But the joke's on you, Shasta. If you're reading this (or having your farmer friend read it to you), you should know that I have a new dog, Gipper. And Gipper is twice the dog you'll ever be. His coat is way shinier than yours, and he doesn't chew up my comic books. And he hates farms. Gipper will never betray me, and he's never going to leave me. He's been right by my side for the last fifteen years, and he'll be there for the next fifty.

So if animals aren't our friends, then what are they?

The answer can be summed up between two buns.

THE FACTORY FARM: AMERICA'S MOST SUCCULENT INDUSTRY

Nation, have you ever wondered how a cow becomes a hamburger? Me neither. I just assumed God did it. But it turns out that food production is actually part of something called Agribusiness. It's this industry that turns cows into steaks, pigs into bacon and everything else into gelatin.

"Everything else" includes, someday, Bill Cosby. (Should have read the fine print.)

THE MIRACLE OF MEAT

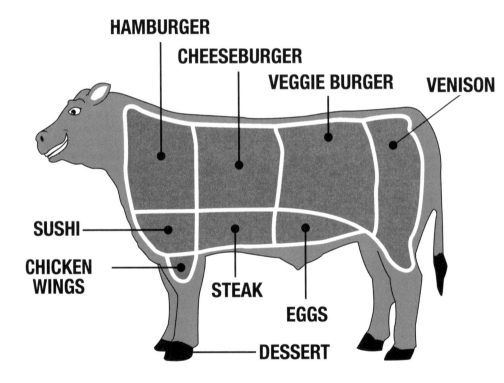

HAMBURGER

CHEESEBURGER

VEGGIE BURGER

VENISON

SUSHI

CHICKEN WINGS

STEAK

EGGS

DESSERT

THE U.S.D.A. AND Y.O.U.

Agribusiness in the United States is overseen by the United States Department of Agriculture. Translation: just more Big Government interference. Hey, if I want to buy meat out of the trunk of some guy's car, that's my business. My *Agribusiness*.

Just one "n" away from Angry-Business!

Here's my second problem. The food pyramid. There is no greater friend of the State of Israel than Yours Truly, and I for one believe it is criminal that the USDA would use an army of Jewish slaves to build these monuments just so school kids can be force-fed the Whole Grain Agenda.

HEY PHAROAH TUTEN-RAMEN-NOODLE!

LET MY PEOPLE GO-GURT!

WHO CARES?

Upton Sinclair wrote a pro-labor book about the Chicago stockyards called *The Jungle* that pointed out minor flaws in the meat industry, such as the frequency of severed limbs. Big deal. I knew an accountant who got his arm chopped off in a filing cabinet. But you'll never hear about that in a book.

He kept the arm and claimed it as a dependent.

Truth is, Upton Sinclair was a Socialist, which means what he really wanted was for cattle to control the distribution of wealth. One guess who *they'd* give it to.

THE TRUTH: IT'S WHAT'S FOR DINNER.

Now some people complain that the factory scale of Agribusiness means cruelty to animals, environmental destruction, and meat loaded with chemicals and hormones.

But they're not awarding any points for the fact that on the factory farm, a cow can go from mooing to stewing in under ninety seconds.

READY, PET, GO!

Okay. Now that I've pulled the wool off your eyes about animals, you're ready to get one and establish the proper dominant relationship.

It's important to select the right animal. Different lifestyles call for different pets to master. If you're away from your home a lot, you may want to boss around a cat. If you don't like to exercise, consider lording over an iguana or perhaps a weak-willed parakeet. But if you do have the time to dedicate, there is no beast more satisfying to dominate than the dog.

If you want to be a real asshole, get a ferret.

Once you've selected a pet and named it, it's time to bend the animal to your will. I've done this with my dog Gipper by teaching him a few authoritative commands, such as SIT. When I order Gipper to sit, I'm letting him know that I am his superior. Of course, Gipper has a bad back, so after I ask him to sit, I massage his hindquarters while I ease him onto a pillow.

> **What's on Top of a House?** It's "roof." Not "ruff."
> Make sure your dog says "roof."

Just like with humans, dogs determine what type of person you are by the firmness of your handshake. If you have a strong grip, they'll respect you. If you have a weak grip, they'll turn your neck into a chew toy. So be sure to give your dog's paw a hearty squeeze and NEVER break eye contact. Of course, my dog Gipper doesn't like to be touched, so when I ask him to shake, I bow to him Japanese-style while averting my gaze.

For Masonic dogs, try clutching the elbow.

THE DE-BALLIFICATION OF THE AMERICAN PETSCAPE

Anyone who has ever spent $5 to purchase a newborn dachshund out of a cardboard box in a supermarket parking lot knows the joy of a litter of puppies. Without them the desk calendars of our nation's secretaries would be blank.

Don't let someone else's pets read this book. Have your animal mark its territory:

HERE

But there is a movement afoot in this country, spearheaded by certain octogenarian game show hosts, to spay and neuter our pets, ostensibly to control their population. Instead of letting animals be animals these people choose to "Cut and Run."[2]

At its very core, this scissor-happy movement is an affront to virility and is brazenly anti-ball. Think of the agony you put your neutered dog through when, during a simple game of fetch, you ask him to chase down and retrieve a symbol of his lost manhood. The Anti-Cruelty Society is performing these procedures![3] And they say irony is dead!

Apparently it's just playing, 'possum

Worst of all, neutering is birth control, plain and simple. Instead of the wholesale de-sacking of these creatures, we should be promoting abstinence education for our pets. They will get the same satisfaction teenagers do from remaining chaste until they are married. And yes, I am once again advocating animal marriages.

*Not animal **gay** marriages!*

---

[2] *A major weapon in the War on Testicles is language. What do we call the offspring of our cats and dogs? Not a "Bounty" or a "Blessing" but a "Litter"!*
[3] *One minute they're telling you how important it is to save some endangered species no one has ever heard of, the next they're begging you to neuter your pets. Which is it, more animals or less? You can't have your Spotted Owl[4] and eat it too.*
[4] *For the record, delicious.*

ON ENDANGERED SPECIES

To put it simply, certain animals are endangered because God is pissed off at them. If you try to save an endangered animal, you are going against God's will—and the Man knows how to hold a grudge.

ENDANGERED ANIMALS
and
WHY THEY ARE UNLOVED BY GOD

Florida Cougar
(Puma Concolor Coryi)

Laziness. Where's the challenge in hunting slow, elderly prey?

California Condor
(Gymnogyps californianus)

Typical West Coast type just cruising on the air currents. Get a job, long beak.

Hawaiian Monk Seal
(Monachus schauinslandi)

Despite name, not really a devout member of a monastic order.

Ocelot
(Leopardus pardalis)

It knows good and well what it did.

Père David's Deer
(Elaphurus davidianus)

Has an accent mark in its name.

Bighorn Sheep
(Ovis canadensis)

Wool can only be washed on "delicate" cycle, if you know what I mean.

Iberian Lynx
(Lynx pardinus)

Agnostic.

Hairy-Nosed Wombat
(Lasiorhinus krefftii)

Unloveable.

I Went to the Zoo Once: Not impressed. The animals were lazy. If I want to see a monkey sleeping, I'll tranquilize one. But what do you expect from today's modern zoos? Now every animal has its own habitat—Bear Country, Tiger Mountain, Hedgehog Hotel, Baboon Condo. It's so safe and sterile. How are my kids supposed to learn anything about nature if the animals aren't savaging one another? I say we put all the animals into one big enclosure and let them battle it out. After all, it's a dog-eat-dog world; so let's have some dogs eating each other. Not my dog Gipper, though. He has a very sensitive stomach.

If I went to a play and all the actors were asleep, I'd get a refund.

STEPHEN SPEAKS FOR ME
A CHANCE FOR AVERAGE AMERICANS TO AGREE WITH WHAT I THINK

L73NR, Cow

I'd like to thank Stephen for the opportunity to put my two cents in here. To be honest, I was hesitant to commit my thoughts to paper. The last thing I want to do is perpetuate the illusion that I actually have thoughts. Dinner doesn't think, and you shouldn't think about your dinner.

Hey, want to hear a funny joke? Cattle prods. I guess you had to be there.

It's just that I don't understand why, after offering me the opportunity to be processed into sirloin, Farmer Joe thinks he needs to twist my hoof. I'm in!

What's that honey? In a minute, Mommy is writing something for a book. That's right! B-O-O-K! Book! Good girl! Now run along and tell your sister it's time for bed. You know, Mohandas Gandhi once said, "The cow is a poem of compassion," but you know what I say? The cow is a rack of short ribs.

Speaking of Gandhi, it's at times like these (approaching the mechanical separators), that I am glad I'm a Hindu. Because I know I have lived a good life and will come back to live again and again until I escape the wheel of Samsara. When I next return, I hope I'm a human. The first thing I'm going to do is have a steak. I'm dying to know what all the fuss is about. You people sure seem eager to get it off my bones. Well I should sign off before I get to the Captive Bolt Stunner.

Enjoy me!

CANARY IN A COAL MINE

Nation, nothing restricts freedom more than buckling a seatbelt. If I want to fly head first through my car windshield at 200 mph, that's between me and my brain damage. But, as long as there are legislators in the pocket of Big Seatbelt, the regulations will keep on coming.

Don't believe me? Take a look at this story from abcnews.com:

BUCKLE UP, PUP

For Massachusetts canines, flatbed freedom and tongues flapping in the breeze on the open road may soon go to the dogs. Martin Walsh, a state lawmaker from Dorchester, Mass., may file legislation that will require dog owners to restrain pets when driving in a vehicle.

A law to make dogs wear seatbelts! What's next, Massachusetts? Making dogs wear hard hats when they chase the ball? Or life vests when they swim in a lake? Or safety goggles when they spot-weld?

Never once did Lassie tell Timmy she wanted more government regulations. "What's that, girl? There's a fire in the old barn? You want me to fill out this paperwork in triplicate and wait for someone from the main branch to contact me in six to eight weeks?" Ridiculous.

 Half the reason the comic strip Marmaduke is so funny is because he's always getting into mischief. If the government starts regulating that mischief with a bunch of unnecessary safety standards, that Great Dane will become a Mediocre Dane. Then where will we turn for entertainment? Cathy? Too highbrow!

Endangered Species

Massachusetts, you've already taken our dogs' balls. Don't take their rights too.

FUN  ZONE

Can you re-ball the boys before Sandy is out of heat?
Draw a line from the missing sack to the right breed!

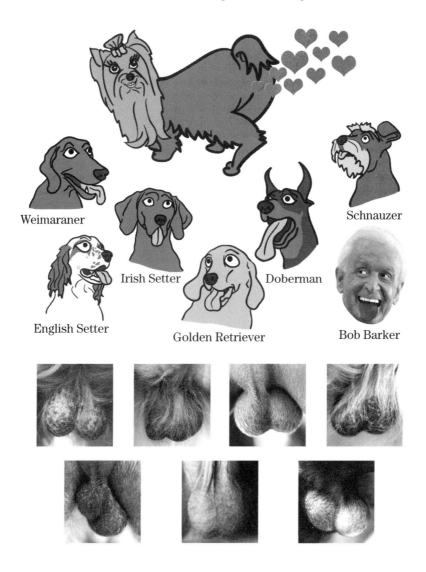

fig 6. STEPHEN COLBERT

★ ★ ★

CHAPTER 4

RELIGION

"Jesus is just all right with me."
–The Doobie Brothers
But are they all right with Jesus? Drop the reefer, boys, and pick up a Bible!

 **NEWS FOR THE GODLESS: RELIGION IS INESCAPABLE. THERE HAS NEVER BEEN A HUMAN SOCIETY WITHOUT SOME FORM OF WORSHIP. AND DON'T POINT TO COMMUNIST SOCIETIES LIKE THE SOVIET UNION—THEY WORSHIPPED BLUE JEANS. OF COURSE, BEATNIKS, PEACENIKS, AND NO-GOODNIKS QUESTION**

why we need religion. "Imagine," they croon, "there's no countries. It isn't hard, it's true. Nothing to fight or kill for, and no religion, too." You may find that idea appealing because it rhymes. But so does this: "God said to Noah there's gonna be a floody-floody / Get those children out of the muddy-muddy."

Mine rhymes 4 times.

The "children" mentioned in that Bible verse didn't think they needed religion either, and look what happened to them (drowny-drowny). Bottom line: Religion is the cornerstone of civilization. Without it, we would have no laws, no morality, no social structure, and no guidelines for furnishing our tabernacles. We would exist in a state of valueless depravity, like they do in Holland.[1]

Agriculture is the flying buttress.

---

[1] *Note to Publisher: For Dutch edition, change to "Belgium."*

GOOD NEWS

Religion exists. And so mankind can benefit from its numerous gifts.

Law: The Ten Commandments are the basis of our entire system of justice. Without them we wouldn't have laws, and without laws there'd be chaos.[2] Those two tablets give you everything you need to run an orderly society. Lying, stealing, murdering, adultery, idol worship and coveting are *out*. Parent-honoring and Sabbath observance are *in*. By the way, if you're reading this on your religion's Sabbath, you'd better have a non-believer there turning the pages for you, because when it comes to the T.C.s, I'm an originalist. That means, if a neighbor takes so much as a covetous *glimpse* at my wife, I'm looking for my lucky stoning hat.

I can recommend a good page-man.

It's made of stone (so I blend in).

Morality: Religion lays out clear definitions of good and evil, distinguishing good deeds—"*solids*" in Biblical Hebrew—from sins. Think about it: Without this guidance and reward/punishment system, how would we know that it's actually *good* to give charity to beggars? Plus, without the concept of Right and Wrong, we'd have no cowboy movies or cop shows because there'd be no good guys and bad guys—just guys.

Good & Plenty would just be Plenty.

And forget about karaoke. I mean, "(If Loving You Is Wrong) I Don't Want to Be Right" is my go-to crowd pleaser, but who wants to hear "(If Loving You Is Okay) Then, Okay"?

Social Cohesion: Religion gives communities reasons to come together and build bonds through shared participation in rituals. Admit it—people would never speak to anyone outside their immediate families if not for mandatory pilgrimages to holy rocks or watching virgins' hearts get carved out atop their ziggurats.

Witch trials make great mixers.

I know what a ziggurat is.

Hope: I believe it was the tiger-philosopher Hobbes who described human life as "solitary, poor, nasty, brutish, and short." Religion allows us to ignore all that by praying. When we appeal to our deities with a slaughtered ewe, or prostration, or, in the case of Hare Krishnas, airport conga line, we exert some control over our existence and are filled with hope that God may improve it. Otherwise, we're just chanting our deepest desires into a silent, indifferent void. How depressing would that be?

---

46   [2] *On the plus side, you wouldn't get a $100 ticket for parking in front of your own TV studio for, like, **thirty seconds**. C'mon!*

Meaning: Life is chaotic and unpredictable. If a butterfly flaps its wings in one part of the world, it could cause people at the opposite end of the globe to watch a Discovery Channel special on butterflies. And what's on next? A show about tornadoes. Who made such a harrowing program schedule full of seemingly random destruction? It was God's will.

Moths, get a publicist.

Responsibility: Religion forces every individual to take responsibility. Specifically, take it away from yourself and give it to God. If we had to be accountable for every one of our actions, we'd be crippled with indecision. But with religion pointing the way, we can feel confident in our choice to picket our children's elementary school when we find out the art teacher is gay.

Hi, Mr. Jellineck!

Immortality: If you're good, you don't "die." It's my favorite gift of religion, because it's the most practical. For instance, I got that PBS *Civil War* series on DVDs last Christmas but I haven't had time to watch. (I can't wait to see how it turns out.) But thanks to religion, after I depart my earthly body I'll have eternity to watch those DVDs with Abraham Lincoln. He ought to be able to tell me if Ken Burns[3] got it right.

So, now that you understand religion's gifts, you can understand why America chose to be a Godly nation, and by Godly I mean Jesusly.

RELIGION IN AMERICA

Make no mistake: America is a Christian nation. The bedrock of our theo-democracy is our Judeo-Christian Values™. That term, by the way, is a bit of a misnomer. It implies that Christianity and Judaism are equal. That makes about as much sense as comparing Jesus to Moses. One of them could walk <u>on</u> water; the other one had to <u>part</u> it. Which one seems more Christian to you? Think of "Judeo-Christian" like "Sears, Roebuck & Co."—Judaism is Roebuck.

The "& Co."? Unitarians.

Now, the Secular-Progressives out there are going to say, "Hold on, Colbert. Wasn't America founded on the ideas of Enlightenment thinkers like Hume and Paine?" Common misconception. Who landed at Plymouth Rock? Pilgrims. And the only reason they got on the *Mayflower* was to flee religious persecu- tion. That means they had a religion: Christianity. And thank God they did. If it wasn't for Jesus' message of love in their hearts, do you think they would have taught the Indians that "maize" is really called "corn"?

Thank you, Jesus.

---

[3] *Once again, a reporter who failed to interview anybody **who was actually there.***

> **GUT-CHECK:** Since the Pilgrims were victims of persecution, some assume they were tolerant. That's just liberal propaganda. Sure, they were against persecution…of Pilgrims. But after they changed their name to "Puritans" (in what I believe was a copyright dispute), they were more than happy to drown what Lesbians now call Wiccans.

??????

We hear a lot about how the founders created a so-called "wall of separation between church and state." The myth of such a wall is exacerbated by our Constitution's confusingly worded First Amendment:

Pat Robertson, tear down this wall!

"Congress shall make no law respecting an establishment of religion…"

Many point to these words as somehow prohibiting the establishment of Christianity as our national religion. But if the founders were so anti-Christian, how come the Constitution never mentions evolution?

It's not "We the Ape-People."

And even if I'm wrong, just because "Congress shall make no law" doesn't mean that we can't establish a religion. It just means we'll have to do it without Congress. An executive order, perhaps?

Or just a knowing wink

So, to sum up: America is a Christian nation. And as the old Negro spiritual says, "This Train is bound for Glory, this Train." Folks, America is riding the Jesus Train.

Attention travelers: Please note that the Jesus Train is NOT the Crazy Train or the Night Train or the Midnight Train to Georgia. There's a big difference. Check your tickets before boarding.

JESUS TRAIN TIMETABLE

	 Jesus Train	 Crazy Train	 Night Train	 Midnight Train to Georgia
Origin	Manger	Bum-bum! Bum-bum, bum-bum, bum-bum! Ay! Ay! Ay!	7-11	L.A.
Destination	Salvation	Off the rails	Oblivion	Georgia
Departure Time	Rapture	Next full moon?	As soon as enough change is collected	Midnight
Onboard amenities	Bliss, eternal life, moral certitude	Bum-bum deedle-deedle deedle buh-duh buh-duh buh-duh-buh-duh bum-bum	Sleep and/or pee anywhere you want	Pips
Meals	Manna from Heaven	Dove, bat	None (it's coming back up anyway)	Roast beef sandwich ($11.99?!)

One Other Thing: Just because you're on a God Train doesn't mean you're bound for Glory. Only Our Lord's locomotive will carry us to the winner's circle, but don't take my word for it. Let our God's record speak for Itself.

HOLY WAR. HUH! WHAT IS IT GOOD FOR? ABSOLUTELY EVERYTHING.

Training and equipping fighting men in the field goes a long way to winning any armed conflict. But if you really want to tip the scales in your favor, get God on your side.[4]

And have Him bring Air Power

Look no further than the words of Lieutenant General William G. Boykin, U.S. Deputy Undersecretary of Defense for Intelligence, who described our victories over our terrorist enemy thusly: "I knew my God was bigger than his. I knew that my God was a real God and his was an idol."

A big Salaam aleichem to my Muslim fans!

That should be carved into the lead of every bullet fired out of every American gun. Too long to fit, though. How about this:

"My God can beat up your god."

Because He can! Take a look.

THE OFFICIAL WIN-LOSS RECORD OF THE JUDEO-CHRISTIAN GOD

The War in Heaven (Lucifer's Rebellion)

Calculations courtesy Pope John XXI (c. 1273 AD)

Lucifer leads 133,306,668 fallen angels against God's 266,613,336 good angels. Not surprisingly, God wins, because God was on God's side.
God: 1, Not-God: 0.

Israelites vs. Canaanites

Have they tried blowing a trumpet in Iraq?

Joshua blows a trumpet, and the walls of Jericho fall. Later, the sun stands still at Gibeon and the moon in the valley of Aijalon so the Israelites can defeat the Amorite kings. But maybe the atheists are right—maybe it was all just a coincidence.[5]
God: 2, Not-God: 0.

The Crusades

The Crusades lead to the Knights Templar; the Knights Templar lead to the Masons; and the Masons lead to the Shriners, a secret society that controls world governments, toys with our banking system, and single-handedly keeps the fez industry afloat. I'd say God won this round.
God: 3, Not-God: 0

---

50 [4] *Or a team of exiled Jewish physicists. Those guys really had a bee in their bonnet about something.*
[5] *If you believe that, I've got some swampland in the Kingdom of Reuben to sell you!*

The Hundred Years' War

With God's help, King Henry V wins the decisive battle at Agincourt in 1415 against the idolatrous French, giving the English control of the north and west of France.

God: 4, Not-God: 0.

Terrible name for a war. **Never set a date for withdrawal.**

The Hundred Years' War II

With God's help, Joan of Arc lifts England's siege of Orleans, giving the French control of the north and west of France.

God: 5, Not-God: 0.

The Fall of Constantinople

When the Muslims took over Constantinople in 1453, it wasn't because God was on the Ottoman Empire's side. He was just mad at the Byzantines for breaking off from the Catholic Church over the addition of the word *filioque* to the Nicene Creed in 1054. Hey guys, "You schism it, you buy it." Sorry, I'm still a little bitter.

God: 6, Not-God: 0.

We all scream for Nicene!

Revolutionary War

Sorry, Great Britain, but if you go up against "One nation, under God," you're going to get your ass handed to you *twice* as hard. (Historico-linguistical note: At this point, "God" became synonymous with "America.")

God: 7, Not-God: 0.

The Civil War

Since America was on *both* sides, whichever way this thing went, everyone knew it would be a windfall for the Lord.

God: 8, Not-God: 0.

"Brother-against-brother" is another way of "doubling-down."

World War I

God wasn't sure which way to go here—lot of Christians on both sides—so He sat it out for fear of tarnishing His perfect record. But then in 1917 America joined in, so He had no choice. He won it, then retired, making this officially The War to End All Wars.

God: 9, Not-God: 0.

World War II

God got forced out of retirement by the taunting of Japanese Shinto spirit deities. Germany joined with the Japs (bad move by them), and God killed Socialist President Roosevelt so Truman could drop The Bomb.[6]

God: 10, Not-God: 0.

Note: "Jap" is an acceptable term when used to save ink.

Korean War

Technically, not a war—a "police action." Doesn't count. Although you don't see me writing this book in Korean. So, really...

God: 11, Not-God: 0.

Vietnam

You can't say God lost Vietnam. The Democratic Congress lost it, by refusing to fund God's war. He may be omnipotent, but He's not made out of money.

God: 11, Not-God: 0, Democrats: -1.

You're thinking of Mammon.

Iraq

That's the last time God listens to Rumsfeld.

Once again, God won the War. He just doesn't occupy very well.

God: 12, Not-God: 0, Democrats: -1.

So it's clear that when you follow God, you're riding on the winning train,[7] but if you want to go first class on ChrisTrak, there's only only one way to ride...

---

52 [6] *Some may doubt God's hand here, but do you know what Truman's job was before being President? He* **sold hats.**
[7] *Train races! Why isn't there more of this? We could build parallel tracks, or there could just be time trials. We can figure the specifics out later. Get on this, Amtrak!*

Roman Catholicism!

Jesus founded only One Church and it wasn't Unitarian. He took His apostle Simon and made him into a rock and built a church on *Simon says "Pray!"* him. It's called "the Holy Roman Catholic and Apostolic Church," or "Church" for short.

Catholics have many advantages over other Christians. One is marble. For the buck I put into the collection plate, I want some production value. That means a church, not some community center that doubles as a basketball court.

Also, Catholics have saints—more than 10,000 of them. They're like God's customer service reps, and each of them has a specialty. Say you lose your wallet. You could bother the Creator to help you find it, but if you're a Catholic, you don't have to. Just pray to St. Anthony. Finding lost things is all he does. For Eternity. Also, there are times when you might want to pray to St. Agatha. She's the patron saint of nursing and bell-making. If you're both a nurse and a bell-maker, that's one-stop shopping.

Some are put off by the labyrinthine structure of Catholic dogma, but many of its rituals are quite beautiful, and not just when edited together as a tense, poetic counterpoint to brutal violence in Mafia films.

But maybe you're not ready to be a Roman Catholic. Well, as the saying goes, "There are many roads to God." Some are just more twisty than others. So if you want to get a little needless exercise, why don't you try one of these Goat Paths to Nowhere?

Protestantism

This is a variant form of Christianity, or "heresy."

Protestants don't make me angry as much as disappointed. Unlike *But they do make* the world's crazy made-up religions, they're so close to getting it *me angry.* right. They're a single Pope away from reaching their full potential.[8] But instead of stepping up and making a commitment to one, holy, apostolic Church, they're stuck on this notion of "independence," of unmediated faith in Christ. Do you really think God prefers a mess of polyglot, disorganized prayers over the elegant hand-written Latin epistles from Benedict XVI? As

---

[8] *I'm sure the Pope would put on a polo shirt and boat shoes, if that would make you feel more comfortable.* **53**

if He doesn't have enough to do already without putting your request for an aboveground pool into Babel Fish.

So we get it, Protestants. You've had your 490-year "protest"—let's move on. Martin Luther was probably right to translate the Bible into German, and I'll grant that he may have had a legitimate beef about selling indulgences. But let's stop living in the past. Whenever you're ready, the Church's doors are always open. We'll let you back into eternal salvation, and all you have to do is say a few Hail Marys, feel a little guilty, and deliver us your massive army of lockstep values voters.

*Where I come from, nailing things to a church door is **vandalism**.*

Plus, if you come back into the fold, I've got some bargain-basement relics you might be interested in. I'm talking rare, primo St. Ebrulf shinbone.

It blows.

That's my general take on Protestantism. Here's the blow-by-blow:

Episcopal Church
Why don't Episcopalians just come out and say it: They're Anglicans. A bunch of Tory Loyalist Brit-o-philes living in our midst, just waiting for the day America lets her guard down so they can slip tea into our coffeemakers, bayonet our bald eagles, and reinstate Henry VIII. Let's keep an eye on these people.

Methodism
Don't be a Meth-head.

What, the Church of England wasn't heretical enough for you?

Presbyterians
"Forgive us our debts?" Who are they, Bono?

Presbyterians are identical to Methodists except that one of them says "debts" instead of "trespasses" in the Lord's Prayer. Hundreds of years of bitter armed conflict has failed to resolve this difference. How many more lives must be lost?

Baptists
I'm a pious guy, but even I have my limits. I draw the line right around spending 8 hours in church every Sunday. Church should be a solemn 45 minutes to sit quietly and feel guilty, with donuts at

the end to make you feel better. I don't go in for a full day of singing and dancing and rejoicing, no matter how nice the hats are. I prefer my Gospel monotonously droned to me from a pulpit, thank you very much.

Quakers[9]

These folks produced only two things I like—Oatmeal and Richard Nixon.

Actually the rice cakes aren't bad either.

The Church of Jesus Christ of Latter-Day Saints (Mormonism)

To their credit, Mormonism's founders did something that other self-proclaimed prophets throughout history never thought of: They lived in America. I'll admit it even makes me a bit uncomfortable to think that my doctrine was established somewhere as unseemly as the Middle East.

The Church was founded after prophet Joseph Smith left a lucrative career divining for treasure to find the golden plates containing the Book of Mormon, which describes a visit by Jesus to America after He left Jerusalem. Evidently He was ascending to Heaven, got just above the clouds, and took a hard left.

On the plus side, any guy who's ever agonized over "boxers or briefs" before a hot date should consider Mormonism.[10] They have special underwear, so that decision is made for you. Plus, pre-marital sex is prohibited. Casual sex is really not a problem at all to these guys, even after you're married. The Church wants you to have 11 kids, so sex is never going to be casual. It is going to be *work*.

And I'll give the Mormons this: They know which way the wind blows. When America decided that polygamy wasn't the way to go, the Mormons changed their ways and banned it. They had similar changes in policy when public opinion turned against the traditions

---

9 *Any religion that calls itself "Friends" comes across as a little desperate.*
10 *I recommend a thong. Nothing turns the ladies off more than a visible jockey-line.*

of massacring pioneers and believing that all Black people are evil. Pretty much whenever the general populace decides that Mormons are a sinful crazy cult, their leader receives a message straight from God that makes everything OK. This practice continues to this day; you can see it in the way that Mitt Romney was pro-choice when he was running for governor of Massachusetts, but was divinely inspired to become pro-life when he was running for the Republican nomination for president.

On the minus side, you could be ex-communicated by Donny Osmond.

Judaism

 Now, I have nothing but respect for the Jewish people. Since the Bible is 100% the true Word of God, and the Jews believe in the Old Testament,[11] that means Judaism is 50% right.

My biggest problem with Judaism is its tradition of literary criticism. Its highest ideal is to sit around studying day and night. I can't trust any religion with that kind of book-fetish. As much as I love the Bible, even I can only read so much in one bathroom sitting. Let alone the Talmud. Seriously, Rashi, every tractate needs a commentary? It wouldn't hurt to take a seltzer break once in a while.

Commenting in the margins of books is stupid.

Also, there's this whole notion of "Jewish Guilt." Hmm, sounds familiar. Maybe because it was originally called "Catholic Guilt"! Quit trying to steal our spot as guiltiest religion, Jews. If your mother knew about this blatant theft, it would kill her—*kill* her.

They don't even need the guilt. They've got plenty of other ways to make themselves miserable. Just look at their holidays. The most important one involves spending a day not eating and thinking about all the bad things they've done. You get the day off from work, and you spend it moping. Count me out!

Look, guys, you need to lighten up. I've been to Jewish weddings—I know you can cut loose when you want to. That thing with the chair is crazy. Let's bring around a little more of that.

[11] *Which the Jews call* Matzo.

Also, if you could concentrate on rebuilding that Temple and bringing forth our Armageddon/Second Coming, we'd really appreciate it.

The Rapture is the only way you're getting rid of us.

With their common devotion to the Word of God as revealed in the Old and New Testaments, the Christians and the Jews share a common heritage.[12]

Together these Testaments are known as:

THE BIBLE

It's a big book with big words like Abednego. It's also often misinterpreted. Here's all you need to know.

THE OLD TESTAMENT

After Jesus showed up, the Old Testament basically became a way for Bible publishers to keep their word count up.

Of course, just because Jesus replaces the Old Testament doesn't mean you should necessarily skip it. That would be like skipping *Batman & Robin* just because the story starts over in *Batman Begins*.[13] The important thing to realize is that both the old and the new stories are about an all-powerful being trying to rid the world of evildoers, only in the new one The Batman can eat pork.

Bat-chops!

But in case you don't have time to consult the Old Testament, I've taken the liberty of summing up the highlights below. This isn't supposed to be a replacement for the Old Testament, but if you want to save some shelf-space by tearing it out of the Bible and replacing it with this book, I'm sure God will understand.

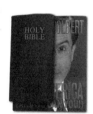

Fine with God.

THE CONCENTRATED OLD TESTAMENT[14]

Creation: "In the beginning, God created the heaven and the earth." Sorry, Darwin-huggers, but it's not "In the beginning, a monkey evolutioned gay marriage."

Adam and Eve/ The Fall of Man: Mankind is inherently sinful. Also inherently trusting of women and snakes. Fight these instincts!

---

[12] *Except for the Jews.*
[13] *Starring **Christ**ian Bale, directed by **Christ**opher Nolan. Coincidence?*
[14] *Just add Jesus.*

Cain and Abel: Are you your brother's keeper? Yes, but that doesn't mean he can live in your guest room forever. Get a <u>job</u>, Allen!

Noah and the Flood: All weather is sin-related. Lust causes thunder, anger causes fog, and you don't want to know what causes dew.

Dew-ing it

Sodom and Gomorrah: If you wonder what God thinks about sodomy, just ask a Sodomite. Oh, that's right—you can't, because God destroyed them all with fire and brimstone.

The 10 Commandments: Moses' greatest achievement, though that beard was a close second.

David and Goliath: Size doesn't matter, but temperature does. Come on, put on some pants!

King David and his "slingshot"

Book of Job: Bad things happen to good people. Suck it up.

Jonah swallowed by a whale: If you don't run away from your responsibilities and you never tell a lie, one day you'll become a real boy.

Samson and Delilah: Don't let your girlfriend cut your hair!

THE NEW TESTAMENT
Spoiler Alert! Jesus is the salvation of all mankind.

OTHER HEATHENS
Shinto

Shinto is a Japanese religion based on the worship of *kami,* or spirits, which inhabit everything. So any object or concept you want to pray to, you can. Sometimes the kami are even stacked up double: For example, each tree has a kami in it, but then there's another kami for all trees. So, first strike against this bull-Shint? It's inefficient. I could probably run that religion with half its current spirit workforce. And those savings would get passed directly to the believer.

Provided none are illegal immigrant spirits

Plus, a whole bunch of magical beings based in different parts of nature? That's not a religion, that's Pokemon. Which shows how Shinto hooks you—once you've prayed to a few spirits, you've "gotta catch 'em all!"

Hinduism

I'm torn on Hinduism. On the one hand, they believe in karma and reincarnation, where good things happen to people who do good deeds and bad things happen to people who do bad deeds. Then after you die, they take a look at your karma account and you come back as something better or worse, depending on how you did. I like this philosophy, because it means if you're good enough in this life, you can be reincarnated as a Catholic. And if this stuff is true, I was one amazing Hindu in my last life. And given the amount of good I'm doing now, it's Next Stop: Nirvanaville for me.

A god, or whatever

Also, Hindu gods make fantastic stuffed animals. They've got us there. When it comes to merchandising, the Catholic Church doesn't have anything to compete with a blue elephant head.[15]

But there's plenty to be worried about. First off, they got us in the numbers game. There are <u>how</u> many people in India who worship <u>how</u> many gods with <u>how</u> many arms? Multiply all that together, and the results are truly terrifying. What worries me more is their injunction against beef. There's nothing more mouth-watering than a strong, healthy bovine in the artificial-hormone-induced prime of life. So what if it could be my great-grandfather reincarnated? I'd be honored to pass through the colon of my descendants. Give me a break.

Worst beanie
baby ever.

Buddhism

Another go-figure religion. "Hey, why don't we all put on robes and sit in a rock garden and just, like, be *aware*?" Exactly. That's the easiest rhetorical question I've ever asked. Buddhism instructs its followers to forsake attachment to material things. Go for it, guys. That's just more material things for those of us who have enough sense to glorify our Lord with speedboats.

Hey, Buddhists—
this book is a thing.

And frankly, I'm offended by this idea of the so-called "middle way," the Buddhist doctrine of avoiding extremes. What's the point of religion without extremes? You're either a believer who's guaranteed a seat at God's right hand in the Kingdom of Heaven or an infidel condemned to boil eternally in a lake of searing excrement. We're at Holy War; pick a side, tubby.

Buddhists hate
Mountain Dew!

---

[15] *The Hindus have an elephant-headed god Ganesha, and I'll grant it's hard not to worship a deity that can eat hay without using its fingers.*

Islam[16]

Islam is a great and true religion revealed in the Holy Koran which was dictated by the angel Gabriel to the final prophet Mohammed, Blessing and Peace Be Upon Him.

Scientology

This fast-growing but controversial religion is attracting some smart people. At least they seem smart—they certainly know a lot about Scientology!

I know a lot of folks are quick to criticize Scientology for its secrecy and willingness to sue dissenters, but if you figured out the secret to expunging Engrams from the Reactive Mind, you'd be protective of it, too.

Glib

Though I may disagree with Scientology on a number of things—like the notion that Galactic Lord Xenu exiled Thetans to Earth in spaceships shaped exactly like late 60s-era DC-8 airplanes, and then stacked them around volcanoes and blew them up with hydrogen bombs 75 million years ago, and the spirits of these Thetans now inhabit our human bodies and prevent us from reaching our full potential—I do agree with their well-publicized disdain for psychoanalysis. Three hundred bucks an hour and all the guy wants to do is talk about my mother? Beam me up, L. Ron!

Rastafarianism

Any religion that sees 20th century Ethiopian emperor Haile Selassie[17] as a member of the Holy Trinity is worth our suspicion. Then again, any religion whose messiah's name isn't recognized by Microsoft Word can't be that much of a threat. My main beef with these folks is that they try to make smoking grass acceptable by labeling it a "sacrament." In my book, that gets you Raptured right into federal prison camp.

No potato salad, no cry

Still, Reggae is pretty good. Makes great background music at the corporate barbecue.

---

[16] *Islam is a great and true religion revealed in the Holy Koran which was dictated by the angel Gabriel to the final prophet Mohammed, Blessing and Peace Be Upon Him.*
[17] *Member of the Holy Trinity and he couldn't even beat Italy?*

All Other Crazy Cults

The problem with cults is that they don't have the brass to be honest from the get-go. They hide behind phrases like "self-improvement workshop" or "human potential coach" or "improv class," then they slowly sneak in the crazy stuff so that you don't notice. If they had any guts, in the very first cult meeting they'd say, "You all need to wear yellow bedsheets and have sex with me twice a day until we get beamed up to a comet in twelve years. Also, give me all your money."[18] Then we wouldn't have a problem—the wacky people can still join, and the people who are just suggestible can go, "Oh, this is a cult" and get out of there. I'm not trying to take away anyone's right to get poisoned in order to send their spirit to Pluto, I'm just saying they should know what they're getting ahead of time.

Buy I Am America, the audio-book.

Here's an easy way to figure out if you're in a cult: If you're wondering whether you're in a cult, the answer is yes.

Atheists

These No-goodnik no-Godniks are growing in numbers and power in America. It makes me wonder how a God could exist Who'd allow people to piss me off so much.

Luckily, a recent survey published in the *American Sociological Review* revealed that atheists are the least trusted group in America—less trusted, even, than homosexuals. It makes sense—at least we trust the homosexuals with our hair.

*"Dust in the Wind" is **not** a hymn.*

But here's the biggest head-scratcher of all: Not only are atheists destroying our country, they're completely deluding themselves. There's simply no way to prove that there is no God. If I didn't hate them so much, I'd feel bad for these folks. Imagine going through life completely duped into thinking that there's no invisible, omniscient higher power guiding every action on Earth. It's just so arbitrary! Can't they see?

What's worse is that atheists blindly follow whatever their scientists tell them to, no matter how unbelievably fantastical it sounds to rational ears. Yeah, earthquakes are caused by the shifting of giant unseen plates buried deep beneath the ground. There's no way it could be God jiggling the globe because

---

[18] *The Colbert Empowerment System is different. It's not a cult, it's a Mind Management System™ that removes "the unwanted cash that's holding you back."*

people in California commit sodomy. No, that would be too simple!

Atheists enrage me precisely because they impute everything that happens to the semi-random workings of the natural world. They refuse to take responsibility for their actions! If their dog dies, it's because the decay of its cells caused by the aging process was "meant to be." They'll never stand up and say, "I deserved this as punishment for mixing my meats and cheeses." Makes me angry just thinking about it.

Agnostics

 Atheists without balls.

ATHEISTS AND THE BIG SECULAR AGENDA

People of faith like you and me are under attack. Especially people like me.

Atheists are the driving force behind what I call Big Secularism.

Card-carrying members of BS have snaked their way into every branch of our federal government, except for the judicial and executive. Did you know that in the House of Representatives and the Senate, there are as many as *one* self-described atheist currently serving? Democratic Representative Pete Stark of California's 13th district, to name just one. Just think of it—how are any pro-faith initiatives going to make it into law when Congress is held hostage by the anti-God caucus of Stark, his self and him?

BS is a gathering storm—a growing movement of lefty Lord-loathers intent on driving religion out of the public square, no matter how much time I spend hanging tinsel.

🔔 THE WAR ON CHRISTMAS 🔔

I'm not afraid to say it: I love Christmas.[15] Call me crazy, but I like getting together with the family, having a nice meal and opening presents. I even like eating candy out of a sock. I wish there were more days designated to do that. Sorry if that offends some of you, but I promised I was going to tell it like it is. And I'm what you call a Christmas Guy.

How about Thanksgiving dinner out of a sock?

[15] *However, I can't say I love Easter. Pastel colors wash me out.*

That's why it upset me so much when the town hall in the coastal Connecticut hamlet where I vacation was forced to take down its nativity scene. And this is despite the fact that it also displayed a sign telling people they could see a menorah two towns over. But balance isn't what the wall-of-separation-between-church-and-state-huggers are after. They just want to marginalize people of faith of all kinds and push us into the corners of American Life. So, down the display came. It's easy to imagine this sort of thing is happening everywhere. Where will it end?

A Visit from St. Secular

'Twas the night before Christmas, and all through the house
Not a creature was stirring, not even a mouse;
Mamma in her kerchief, and I in the nude,
Were shocked that our holiday had been misconstrued,
When out on the lawn there arose such a clatter,
I sprang from the bed to see what was the matter.
(Mind you, I'm still nude.)
Out to the lawn in my glory, I flew.
To see my manger disassembled by the ACLU.
      –Written by Clement C. Moore, 1822
      –Updated by Stephen Colbert, 2007

Still nude

Imagine a time in the not-too-distant future—December 24th, but instead of festive lights and glowing Santas, the streets are illuminated by police helicopters. Meanwhile, in the streets, roving gangs of children terrorize the city. They have zero respect for authority because whether a child is naughty or nice, everyone gets the same thing for Christmas: Jack Squat. So they've gone wild. It's like Devil's Night in Detroit, only there's still stuff worth burning. As the fires rage, bands of depressed alcoholic derelicts, once jolly carolers, shuffle aimlessly, no longer sharing their cheerful seasonal hymns, but instead searching for a death that will never come. God rest ye, merry Gentlemen. And of course, now that there's no Christmas, insects have grown to enormous size. So everyone has to dodge the ants and beetles that are crushing buses in their powerful mandibles.

The correct answer: no

Does my vision of a world without Christmas sound far-fetched? This is <u>exactly</u> the future the Secul-azis want for your children and grandchildren.

Big Secularism's plan is to keep eroding our holiday. Little by little, they're taking away a manger here, a "Come All Ye Faithful" there, until pretty soon there's nothing left. That's why we've got to dig in our heels and celebrate the holiday bigger than ever. If you usually get one tree, this year get two. If you usually do two, have five. The BSists need to understand that there is no number of trees we are unwilling to cut down to prove our point.

Jesus hasn't forgiven you for that Cross, trees.

EVOLUTION IS REAL!

You heard me! Y'see, there's nothing I like more than using the Big Secularism against itself.

You say Man evolved? Well, Man was made in God's image, so God must have evolved too. I adapted your precious "Ascent of Man" chart to a higher purpose:

How does it feel now, Secularists? You can't possibly argue with this— because it's *your* theory. Based on this chart, Jesus clearly adapted over time to take on attributes that would help Him send you to Hell. In your monkey-evolved faces!

God
Maker of All that Is
Seen and Unseen

I think it's wonderful that Stephen has written such a considerate chapter on Me. Hopefully these pages will decrease the number of skeptics out there, though I understand why some people are atheists and agnostics. It's not going to spare them the Eternal torment of Hell, but I understand. Hey, my fault for giving you all Free Will.

I could convince everybody that I exist by stepping up the Divine Interventions, but there are only so many hours in the day, you know?

This gets to the main question that everyone usually asks Me: If I'm so all-powerful, why don't I answer everyone's prayers? The answer: I used to.

Back in the day, fewer people prayed for me to do things for them. There was a lot more thanksgiving, and it's less time-consuming to answer prayers that are praising you for things. Those were the good old days. Now it's gimme, gimme, gimme.

It especially shows up in sports. Used to be, you never had both sides pray for victory. One team max, and 9 times out of 10 that team was Notre Dame. Now, you're guaranteed to have counteracting prayers. What am I supposed to do? For Me, it's literally a no-win situation. I usually have no choice but to answer the prayer of whichever team is better.

Of course, I can't get caught playing favorites. So if I do help a team, it's not going to be with something cool and dramatic like a line drive that suddenly lifts up and carries over the fence. Instead, I usually just go back in time and make the winning team have practiced more.

I mean, if there's one team that is clearly more righteous, yes, I'll help that team, although sometimes I'll help the team of sinners instead because I love a good underdog. Plus that nudge might set them on the righteous path, or there could be a sick kid, or there's some other factor... you know what? It's complicated. You'd really have to be Everywhere.

Oh, and let me say this—if I have money on a game, I never help either team. No exceptions.

So, in regular life, why do I answer some prayers and not other prayers? Pretty much the same reasoning as sports. Do I return the runaway to her family, or do I get that guy his dream job? (Yes, I do pair up all prayers.)

It's not totally random. I have a system, although I can't really explain it in a way that will make sense to someone without Ultimate Knowledge. Put it this way: If I've helped you find your car keys 20 times, don't bother calling Me when you get a tumor.

You guys in the USA don't know how good you have it. Your nation is crazy blessed already. When the Dow breaks 14,000—that's a mudslide in Guatemala. So, you know, try to keep it in perspective.

And by the way, I always have money on the Super Bowl and the Kentucky Derby, so don't waste your breath.

FUN ZONE

Religious conversion is a rigorous, demanding process designed to test your resolve and dedication to the new faith you've chosen. Or you could just use my **Religion Randomizer**! Because let's face it, if it ain't **Christianity**, it's just Path-to-Hell Lotto!

Go to **www.colbertnation.com** and click on the **Religionizer** button to pick your spiritual poison.

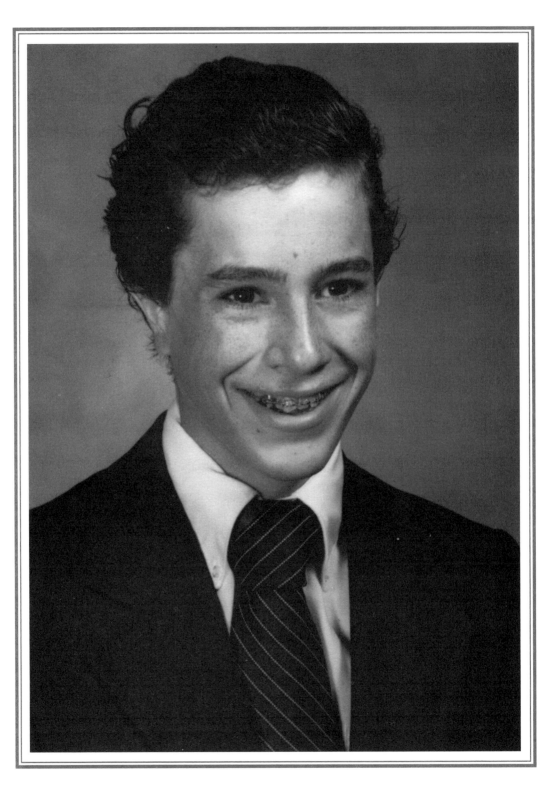

Part Two

MY AMERICAN ADOLESCENCE

★ ★ ★

I was thirteen when we moved from the dirt road where I grew up to the big city of Charleston, where the rich kids lived—kids whose families had been there since it had been Charles Towne or, even earlier, Chuck Mound.

My new school gave me an opportunity I never had before—getting beaten up every day. On those rare days when I was not beaten, the next morning I'd find a note in my locker: "Sorry we forgot to beat you yesterday. We'll beat you twice as hard today." No one can touch Southerners for manners.

The daily beatings lost some of their intensity during the football season, when my jock tormentors were able to split their latent Homosexual Rage between my torso and their locker-room hijinks. This lull allowed my swelling to go down, and it turned out I had facial features. The girls noticed. Soon I was a regular on the debutante circuit where I tried scoring a few "touchdowns" of my own. The beatings began again. Some of those debs were pretty tough.

When I left for college, I was determined never to be a victim again. I would take my lead from the Hollywood tough guys I had always looked up to: Charles Bronson, Clint Eastwood, Ned Beatty. So on Day One of my freshman year at Dartmouth, I walked into class and punched the first person I saw—my Ethics professor, Dr. Buneta. Judging by the grade he gave me, holding a grudge passes for "ethical" in the Ivy League. I don't know what the big deal was. That beard had to absorb some of the impact.

I include this coming-of-age tale because it encompasses the five big Ss of Adolescence:

School, Sports, Sex, Sodomy, and the Silver Screen.

Trust me, they're all in there.

fig 7. STEPHEN COLBERT

★ ★ ★

CHAPTER 5

SPORTS

"No time for losers, 'cause we are the Champions...of the World"

–Freddy Mercury, Glam Rock God and sports *queen*

 **GENERALLY SPEAKING, I'M NOT A BIG FAN OF SPORTS. IT'S A WASTE OF BOTH TESTOSTERONE AND BLIND, FERVENT ALLEGIANCE, BOTH OF WHICH WOULD BE BETTER DIRECTED TOWARDS OUR MILITARY. BUT THERE IS NO QUESTION THAT SPORTS IS A HUGE PART OF OUR CULTURE THESE DAYS. THERE ARE**

dozens of TV channels devoted exclusively to sports—channels you can't remove from your cable package and stop paying for, even if you make it clear that's what you want.

Respond to my letters, Comcast!

So, if I'm no cheerleader of sports, why write a chapter about it? Sports do have some positive impact on society. They solve problems, such as how to get inner-city kids to spend $175 on shoes. They serve as a backdrop for some of our most memorable commercials. And they remain the one and only relevant application of math. Not only that, but we have sports to thank for most of the last century's advances in manliness. The system starts in school, where gym class separates the men from the boys. Then those men are taught to be winners, or at least, losers that hate themselves.

Nothing puts hair on your chest like shame.

ALSO: another great aspect of sports is the chance to share experience with the common man. To see the roar of the crowd from your soundproof skybox, tossing down the vintage port and veal medallions, then rubbing elbows at the post-game locker room party with all your favorite athletes—it's a classic American experience.

Shaq, I must get that recipe for Key Lime Pie!

Speaking of stadiums, I've followed the lead of the team owners and sold the naming rights of this chapter to the highest bidder. So from here on out, this chapter will be known as the...

Chevron

Visit our Sponsor!

CHEVRON:
"The Gas with Techron"
SPORTS CHAPTER

So whether I like it or not, sports are here to stay. And if they're going to exist, I should give them a chapter. Like I always say: if you're not going to listen to me and not do something anyway, at least listen to me and do it right.

> **WAKE UP CALL:** Sorry there, handball, but you're just tennis for poor people.

HISTORY LESSON

Modern "sports" as we know them originated in ancient Rome,[1] when civic officials realized that it would be much easier to get contestants for their gladiator contests if the loser was not killed. Once everyone realized that a live loser could be humiliated for much longer than a dead one, the idea caught on.

Back then, a sport was only what could be achieved with the human body— how fast can you run, how far can you throw, how big a thing can you lift, or push, or kill. But the ideal of sports as an exhibition of human accomplishment ended in 1893 when they started using football helmets. In my book, drawing the impact away from your skull defeats the entire purpose of hitting something with your head.

It's concussion, not con-cushion. Toughen up!

---

72 [1] *Some Ivy Leaguers claim that sports, in fact, originated in Ancient Greece. But athletes back then were nude men covered in oil, which means that the Ancient Greek sports were pretty gay, and therefore, not sports "as we know them." There are no gays in modern sports, with the one exception being all of women's sports.*

> **RULES OF THE GAME:** Sports contain a lot of rules, and I'm not a fan of "rules," especially when it comes to sports. That's just Big Government interference. Let the free market decide what constitutes a touchdown.

Chevron, sponsoring this chapter was a home run!

SPORTS IN THE NEW MILLENNIUM

The big story in sports right now is athletes taking drugs, making themselves better with steroids and human growth hormone. Some people have a problem with this, but not me.

> **NEWS FLASH:** Athletes perform for our enjoyment. So "performance-enhancing drugs" are really "enjoyment-enhancing drugs."

Bravo, Mr. Bonds.

The fact is, Americans want the best of everything. That's why Americans won't watch women's basketball. Every time I see a lady make a shot I think, "I bet a guy could've made that better." "Enhanced" athletics are the same way.

Back in the day when sports consisted of little slow guys hitting set shots, bunting, and staging Statue of Liberty plays, the public was satisfied because they didn't know any better. But now that we've seen huge behemoths with 2% body fat and misshapen foreheads leap over piles of bodies to crush each other's larynx, we can't go back. That's why I'm proposing the end of all regula- *Also no going back post-Black.* tions on what athletes do to themselves. If a guy wants to shoot himself up with hormones or chimp sperm, that's his business. The only thing that matters is performance on the field. Now a lot of people ask, "What kind of message would this send to our young people?" To which I reply, "Don't suck. Go the extra mile to actually be good or you'll be selling insurance." With those forces at work in the marketplace of modern scientific body modification, our sports will continue to be the most entertaining in the world.

TRASH TALK

Sometimes the best performance-enhancing drugs come from the mind. This might come in handy when there aren't any regular performance-enhancing drugs around, or maybe you have them but there's no time to inject. Like when you're in that five-on-five company league hoops game covering the sweaty guy with the mustache and knee brace—let's call him Carl[2]—and he's driving toward the basket and your only options are A) to plant a shoulder in his meaty flank or B) let him score. That's when it's time to let loose with option C) a little trash-talk.

Try this:
"Hey Carl, what's your favorite system of geologically significant caverns? Mine is 'Carlsbad'... at basketball!"

Even during the work day, it's hard to perceive Carl as a human.

Did I need to hit him that hard? Maybe not, but in the heat of after-work coed basketball, you don't always have time to perceive your opponent as a human.

Healthy trash-talk is a vital pillar of the Temple of Sport, and as with the Acropolis its erosion portends the downfall of our civilization.

I'm sure Carl would say the same thing.

"Hey, let's give everyone a trophy, even the kid who never gets put in the game and seems to enjoy himself anyway." That's what Coach PC Police says.

We must stop Carl from mating.

Well, I've got a trophy for that kid, and it's a big bronze boot to commemorate his being kicked out of the league. I don't want my son thinking that mediocrity is an option—"Success or Exposure," that's the Colbert motto. We need to teach our children that their peers are competitors for food, shelter, and eventually mates. And I know I'm not going to win any awards for saying that, probably because these days all the awards have already been given out for "Good Effort."

The scene: Weehawken, New Jersey. A duel between Alexander Hamilton and Aaron Burr. As Hamilton loads his dueling pistol, Burr tells him only fools and mountebanks will use the ten-dollar bill. Hamilton takes umbrage and begins to tell Burr that firstly the ten-dollar bill does not yet exist, and furthermore only dead people can legally appear on U.S. curren...BANG! Welcome to my wallet, Al.

---

[2] *Names have not been changed. If Carl can't handle it maybe he should find another church basement to dribble in. No one drives my lane without paying a toll.*

My favorite places to trash-talk are professional sporting events. Sure, there's no way I could perform at the same level as a professional athlete. But just because I can't beat LeBron James in a dunking contest doesn't mean I can't try and lure him into the stands for a fistfight by pointing out that his trademark headband makes him look like the ringleader of a 1980s exercise video.

SOME PEOPLE are going to say trash-talk is the last refuge of the desperate. You can see these people coming a mile away, in their tweed coats with the *Morning Edition* Travel Mugs. To them I say, "Since when did the spirit of competition become some kind of wet nurse for the weak?" Pointing out an adversary's flaws is a tradition as old as wife-stealing. So, when sporting, never hesitate to dish out heaping servings of hearty smack-pie.

The Blessed Smackrament.

THE SPORTS BREAKDOWN

With the overabundance of sports out there, how do you know which ones to watch? Easy, I'm going to tell you. There are some sports that deserve your respect and adoration and others that should be ignored—I'm looking at you, Soccer. First, let's go over the sports you should be recording nightly on your home Digital Video Recorder.[3]

BASEBALL: Baseball is as American as apple pie. In fact, I've often thought the game should be played with an apple instead of a ball. I have a lot of other great ideas!

For more on my baseball-pie musings, read my book: "Hey Batter, Batter, Batter. Eat Batter."

There's a reason that baseball is the National Pastime, and it's not just because it is our most popular sport, after football, basketball, and NASCAR racing. It is that the simple joy of hitting something with a stick is one that speaks to every American child, regardless of race, class, or upbringing. Wherever there are sticks, or long pieces of processed wood, you can find children hitting something with them. As the child grows, so does the challenge—can you hit something that doesn't want to be hit? And thus begins the child's lifetime love of baseball. Unfortunately, the integrity of the sport has been sullied by our sex-crazed culture. I've heard from a worldly 4th grader that "rounding the bases" is a euphemism for "going all the way" with a girl. Why don't you youths try rounding the abstinence bases instead?

---

[3] *If you wanted me to use your brand name, TiVo, you should have sprung for the sponsorship. I'll say it again, **no free rides**.*

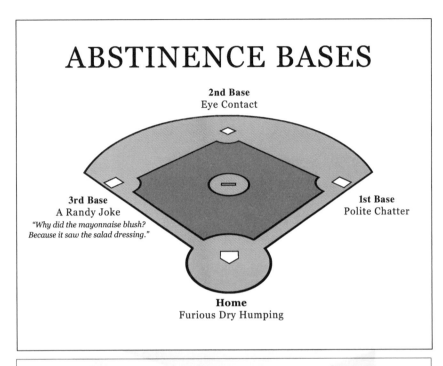

ABSTINENCE BASES

2nd Base
Eye Contact

3rd Base
A Randy Joke
"Why did the mayonnaise blush?
Because it saw the salad dressing."

1st Base
Polite Chatter

Home
Furious Dry Humping

7th INNING STRETCH: "Buy me some peanuts and cracker jacks..." Hey, buy them yourself! Just more melodic proof that we are living in a welfare state.

Baseball reflects the American dream in many other ways. Baseball players are very well paid, and they get to stand around in a park most of the time. Once in a while, a ball comes their way, but the rest of the game can be spent scanning the crowd for hot girls. When their team comes up to bat, baseball players are considered incredibly skilled if they can do their job 35% of the time. In almost all other American professions, workers are expected to get that number up to at least 45% or they'd be fired.

TIME OUT: *Bull Durham* is the best Kevin Costner baseball movie. After that comes *Field of Dreams*, then *For the Love of the Game*, and then *Robin Hood: Prince of Thieves.*

I should add, I do most of my sport-related Kevin Costner research at my local Blockbuster. Why do I tell you this?

BECAUSE: Blockbuster just bought out the sponsorship rights for this chapter from Chevron. It's now called the

BLOCKBUSTER
"Now You Don't Have to Choose"
SPORTS CHAPTER

Ball's in your court, Netflix.

ICE HOCKEY: Ice hockey is training for our eventual war with the glaciers. They've encroached before and they'll do it again. Remember the *Titanic*! This proud sport teaches us how to combat the ice menace using only sticks and a Zamboni. With ice hockey and our good friend global warming, we might just win the cold war again.

Ice, you're on thin ice.

WORLD'S STRONGEST MAN COMPETITION: I've said it before—it's not really a sport unless there's the possibility of dislodging your intestines. Luckily, the Met-Rx World's Strongest Man Competition fits this bill. It uses a complex and indisputable formula to crown its champion. You are truly the most powerful man on earth if you can pull a semi with your teeth, hurl a keg full of lead shot over a wall, and lift at least 20 natives of the impoverished country in which the event is held.[3]

Items you must lift to be the World's Strongest Man:

- A mule
- Rodin's "The Thinker"
- Rodin's 'The Thinker" riding a mule
- A suitcase full of duty-free sambuca
- A train car packed with hobos
- Former Speaker of the House Dennis Hastert
- St. Paul, Minnesota

The one-ton meatball lift is particularly hard.

---

[3] *Every night I carry the weight of the nation on my shoulders. Top that, Iceland's Magnus Ver Magnusson!*

Hey, advertisers, why pay $2 million dollars for a 30-second Super Bowl spot, when you can pay considerably less for an ad here? Think about it.

Are you still thinking about it?

COCKFIGHTING: There's an easy way to tell which came first, the chicken or the egg: Attach a cockspur to both of them and let them fight it out.

My money is on the egg. Those Grade A Jumbos have a lot of attitude.

A good cockpit is a cross between a Thunderdome and a bucket of KFC Snackers™.

If you are lucky enough to get into the sport of cockfighting, I recommend fitting your cock with a Mexican straight blade. It's a much quicker and cleaner kill. The Filipino curved blade is just cruel.

FYI: Due to a last-minute bidding war, this chapter is now called:

THE KRAFT
Seven Seas
Creamy Italian
SPORTS CHAPTER

Please refer to it accordingly.

FIGURE SKATING: Figure skating—including individual and pairs, but excluding ice dancing, figure skating's gay cousin—has everything I could possibly wish for in a sport. Speed, beauty, smooth jazz, sequins, and the chance that someone could at any moment obliterate every tendon in their knees. While it is true that certain Soviet and Chinese people frequently outdo Americans at this sport, that's OK because skating is *all they ever do.*

BASKETBALL: We invented basketball, and it has become so popular that we've developed two versions of it: the college, or "classic," version of the game, in which rules are followed and at most above-average athletes can excel; and the NBA version of the game, in which 7-foot-tall monster freaks leap about on trampolines while swinging their massive elbows like cudgels and running four steps without dribbling before taking off from their opponent's foul line to slam dunk. Each version can be appreciated on its own merits: the NBA for its display of superhuman abilities and larger-than-life personas, and college for its easy-to-understand gambling format. While it's true that Team USA hasn't come in better than 3rd place in most recent World Competitions, that's OK, because the losses are more due to the hubris of our players than their abilities, thus teaching our children a sound moral lesson: If you make enough money in what you do, it doesn't matter if you have your ass handed to you by a Lithuanian.

> **TIME OUT:** Nothing is less American than the Army-Navy game. Whichever side you pick, you're rooting *against* our boys. The Army and Navy squads should be combined, and they should play football against teams from any other country, and instead of footballs they would used bomb-balls. And Air Force can do kickoffs.

FOOTBALL: Football started out as a great idea: "What if we took rugby and got rid of the part where guys stick their heads in each others' butts?" The idea caught on. Soon someone realized that the game would be even more fun if you could throw the ball *forward*. This change took football into its golden age, which continued until they switched over to cowhide. Much of the drama is gone from football these days, as technology has taken over. Plastic helmets have replaced the far more stylish helmets which were less about protecting the head and more about clothing it.

When was the last time you heard of somebody with a leather football helmet getting hurt? Exactly. They work.

SPORTS TO IGNORE

DIVING: Not sure what the big achievement is in walking off the end of a plank and succumbing to gravity. Big deal. To really make the divers demonstrate some skill, the diving events should be held in a zero-G environment like the International Space Station.

Houston, we have a forward somersault pike.

CYCLING: It seems a colossal waste to me to have a dozen cyclists, in peak condition, furiously pedaling their sleek carbon-fiber machines at mind-boggling speeds…and not a single one of them is carrying a takeout order of Chinese food. Because once you're past the age of 12, the only legitimate reason I can think of to get on a bicycle is to deliver someone's steamy container of moo shu pork. I say we limit the cycling events to professional delivery boys and bike messengers, and here's a thrilling twist I came up with the other night while watching *The Road to Perdition*: Each contestant is carrying an envelope he's supposed to deliver to the judge. Inside that envelope: an order to shoot the cyclist dead. The spectators know what's in the notes—the athletes have no idea!!!!

Next to Spandex bike shorts, jean shorts look macho.

Don't tell.

SYNCHRONIZED SWIMMING: I defy you to watch this sport and tell me *I told you to ignore these. Skip Ahead!* the Olympics have no hidden gay agenda, and probably some kind of nose clip kickback scheme going on as well. Besides, a sport in which you win by doing exactly what your partner is doing goes against our American tradition of individuality; it's the aquatic equivalent of the Soviet army marching in lockstep through Red Square, if that army were also wearing women's bathing suits and occasionally twirling in unison. So I reject synchronized swimming, and call instead for it to be replaced by an improvised freestyle underwater dance jam. Still gay, but now American gay.

A QUICK NOTE ABOUT THE OLYMPICS

The Olympics began in perversion: greased up naked men slapping hot sweaty body parts against one another's taut and hairless flesh in pursuit of *Gold Medal Flour, this would be a* victory, like Chippendale's dancers at an after-hours party. And the tradition *great section of the chapter for you to* of perversion[4] continues—because as an international athletic competition, *sub-sponsor.* the Olympics are a warped, watered-down version of the only worthy contest between nations: war.

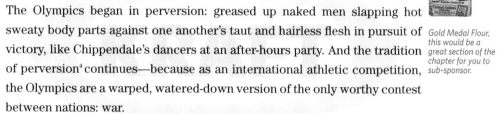

True arguments over international status are not settled by who can throw a fancy hubcap farther. They are settled by invasion. Sure, war takes longer than a 100-meter footrace, but it's much more dramatic, and you don't have to pretend to care about the bronze. Now, I'm not saying that every four years we should have a World War. Such a scenario would play hell with my stock portfolio. I'm simply saying that the modern Olympics should be more <u>like</u> war, in that there should be consequences for winning and losing. The Koreans beat Italy in slalom? They get Michelangelo's David. Rwanda beats Sweden in the high jump? They get to move to Sweden. If Afghanistan defeats us in the biathlon, they can have Connecticut. Warning to you, Connecticut—support our president.

---

[4] *Called a "bi-athlon" for a reason*

FENCING: I like the concept. I don't like the masks, or protective jumpsuits, and for God sake use a real sword, not those effete little French things. I mean, does "epee" sound like something you could open an artery with? You need a blade that wouldn't embarrass a pirate, or maybe one of those martial arts swords that looks like a long walking stick but then when a guy tries to attack you, you pull it apart and whoosh! It's actually <u>two</u> swords. Speaking of martial arts, a few throwing stars couldn't hurt fencing, or any sport for that matter. And can we please get rid of that ridiculous electronic scoring system that uses sensors to tell us someone has made a hit? That's what blood is for.

A LEAGUE OF ONE'S OWN

A NOTE ABOUT WOMEN'S SPORTS: Now I'm not a misogynist, but women have no place in a man's world, especially if that world is profitable sports. Let's leave the multi-million-dollar contracts and rich product endorsements to the big boys and you ladies can stick to the ladylike sports, ones where you can wear skirts such as field hockey or the Scottish caber toss.

Lady like

**The Guy Sitting Next
to You At The Stadium**

They say football is a game of inches, or maybe that's baseball. You know what? Who cares? Because if you care about inches, play horseshoes.

Football is the game I love. That's why I'll brave five-degree weather to stand in a beer line. Those guys are out there playin' for me, the least I can do is show up and drink.

Coming through with beers here! Coming through! Deb, can you grab one? C'mon. Drink fast and keep up with me, because I'm not gonna make extra trips for you in between *my* beer runs. You know *exactly* what I'm talkin' about.

So, why do I love football? Is it because of the action? You bet your sweet derri-ass, but that's only part of the story, because the real game happens in the mind. It's like chess. Kick ooofff! Let's fucking do this! Run, you stupid son of a bitch! Run! Wedge, throw the wedge! Oh, come ooonnnnnn! Deb, you watching this?! What are you doing? Are you kidding me? Who are you talkin' to? What are you talkin' to her for? Fuck Deb, we're at the game, what's with all the talking? Why aren't you drinkin'? You're already behind.

I remember when I was a kid my Dad used to take me to the games. I used to keep a sheet on all the players. I remember all the great ones: Sweetness, Jack "The Assassin" Tatum, "Babalu," "Bucketfoot Al," "Le Demond Blond," "Touchy Taffy," and "Dr. Puntenstein." Those guys gave a hundred and ten percent on the field every Sunday, just so a dad who wasn't home much could have the chance to spend a few hours with his arm around his son sitting on a cold wooden seat sharing a beer. Ohhhhh! Look who they're putting in! Whooo hooo! Pennington. Fucking Pennington! Hey, PENNINGTON! You pretty boy! You whiney country club *pussy*! It's gonna be a long day, Pennington. It's gonna be a looong fuckin' day! Hold on to the ball you bastard! FUUUUUCK! Oh FUMBLE! Get on that BALL! Yeah!! Debbie, look-look. You see that big pile? I hear guys on the bottom of that thing are brutal. Gougin' eyes, grabbin' balls, squeezing balls, bitin' balls. Wait, here comes the ref. What!!! Bullshit! COME ON! *Bullll-Shit, Bullll-Shit, Bullll-Shit!* Yeah, Deb, you got it. *Bullll-Shit!* Did you see that shit?

Hey, so uh Deb, what'd Tricia have to say? What!? I'm just trying to be interested. Jesus, Debbie. No! You're so jealous. Forget it. No, seriously, forget it. Drop it. Jesus, Deb. Jesus. Let's go DE-fense! Let's get a STOP!

Some things don't change for the players, whether they're home or away. When you're on the field, you gotta knock people down, and you gotta put 'em down to stay down. That's it. Easy math. But what does change is, when you're home, you've got the fans. Fans can definitely sway a game. Collectively we're like an extra player. All these people filling up these seats are like my teammates and we are here to rock the house and kick some ass.

Nachos!

What the *fuck* man? You just cashed my *fucking* nachos! I had 'em balanced on the arm rest dipshit, and you rattled the whole row of seats with that fat train of yours! What the fuck are you doin'?! You gonna scoop the cheese off the ground too? No? Well, what the fuck good are nachos without the cheese? I don't care how old he is, if he's so upset, let him cover his fucking ears. What? Go ahead say it again! Say it agoddamngain, go ahead! I don't a give shit, Deb! No, I won't sit down!

I'm gonna get more beer.

Watch out, man. Beers coming through. Sack! Shit, yeah! Did you see that Deb!? How's the turf taste, Sixteen? Huh? How's that taste! You suck! You suck shit! Right Deb?

Some Americans spend their Sundays in church, but football is my religion. This is where I worship, in the house that Lombardi built. INTERCEPTION! Oh-oh-**OH** YEAH! YEAH! GO! GO! YEAHHHHHH! That's what I'm talking about! That's what I'm GODDAMN TALKING ABOUT! Touchdown! High five, Deb! ALRIGHT! You blow, Sixteen! Nice pussy-toss to the wrong team! You gay fag fuck! Whooohoooooooo!

FUN  ZONE

It's customary in the sport of baseball to have the sitting U.S. President throw out the first pitch of the season. Match the former chief of state with his historical toss.

1. After his pitch had catcher stuffed and mounted
2. Handed ball to welfare queen
3. Lobbed two-finger V-sign sinker
4. Used his steam powered mechanical arm to hurl a perfect strike

UNJUMBLE THE HINT
2 RANKLINF DELAON OOSEVELETR　　1 TEDYD ROSOEVELT　　3 CHARDRICH NIXNO　　4 WILLIAM H. TAFT

FUN ZONE: THE INTERACTIVE EDITION

LIAR'S POKER

If ESPN's wall-to-wall coverage of poker is to be believed, lumpy, dour-faced, be-sunglassed middle-aged men are the new Titans of Sport. But 52 cards can be so bulky to carry around in your wallet.

Well, here's a game where all you need are the bills in your pocket. We take turns bidding on the total number of certain digits in the serial numbers found on U.S. currency. The digits are ranked in the following order: 2, 3, 4, 5, 6, 7, 8, 9, 0, 1 (aces). I always play with twenties.

I'll start. I bid five aces. Send me your twenty to see if you've won!

fig 8. **STEPHEN COLBERT**

★ ★ ★

CHAPTER 6

SEX AND DATING

"Feel like makin' love."
–Bad Company, bad influence

SEX!

THAT I HAVE YOUR ATTENTION, I WANT TO TALK ABOUT SEX.[1] IF I HAD TO SUM UP SEX IN ONE WORD, IT WOULD BE THIS ONE: "SEX IS POWER." AND IF I HAD AN EXTRA WORD: "SEX IS A GIFT FROM GOD." BUT BEFORE I GO ON TO THE GOOD STUFF, AND BELIEVE ME THIS CHAPTER GETS STEAMIER THAN A

coed clambake, there's something I have to do. You see, I'm a role model. A lot   *Thank you, Elvis!*
of young folks look up to me. And I don't want to get them into trouble with sex.
So if you're a young person who's not yet married, before reading on, you must
read and sign the following pledge.

---

[1] *You seem a little tense. I give a great massage—maybe that will loosen you up?*

SEX AND DATING CHAPTER PLEDGE FOR UNWED YOUTH

I, the undersigned, pledge to remain sexually abstinent until married to a person of the opposite sex and of legal age. I swear that any knowledge I gain in the following pages regarding human sexuality will be applied only in the private context of a nuptial bed, nuptial kitchen, nuptial bathroom floor, or incorporated into anecdotes to provoke awe in my peers. Should I one day successfully employ any of the information, tips, or techniques provided herein in conjunction with my spouse, I pledge that after a reasonable period of no longer than 24 hours I will credit it/them to Stephen Colbert. So help me God.

Signature of Pledge-Taker: *Notarize here:*

_____

Signature of Pledge-Taker's Parent or Guardian

_____

All right, let's get freaky.

As I mentioned, sex is power—the power to create life, the power to ruin your life, and the power to sex it up good. If you refuse that power, you'll be cheating yourself, and in my case, hundreds of lovely ladies, out of something very special (my penis). But even though sex can be wonderful, it can also be scary, like a maniac, or a haunted house—two things that happen to go great with sex.

Now, before I stimulate you further, I should address a fundamental question: Why do we have sex? I'm on record as preaching abstinence. I talk about it on my TV show, elsewhere in this book, in pamphlets I hand out on street corners, and occasionally in sky-writing. But there is a proper time to have sex: when you want to reproduce. The body parts to which we are attracted are directly linked to child production and nurturing. For men, it's the breasts that provide our offspring nutrition, the legs to which they cling, the lips that kiss the babies goodnight, and the small of the back that teaches our children about the folly of tattoos.[2]

For women, it's the balls. Nothing the ladies love more than a big sack. I mean something a cartoon bandit would carry out of a bank.

Sexy!

Whew. Racy stuff. That poetic description of what a woman yearns for may have heated the blood of some of my female readers, even some of those who signed the abstinence pledge. Remember, you took an oath! So, here's a little scripture sorbet to cool your palate.

> *"It is God's will that you should be sanctified: that you should avoid sexual immorality."*
> —1 Thessalonians 4:3

Exactly. It may be <u>Chad's</u> will that you chug a few wine coolers and drive up to the lake, "'cause it's really beautiful up there," but who are you going to listen to on this one: an omnipotent deity or a management trainee at Outback Steakhouse?

Regional manager, maybe

And for any male readers who found my bandit imagery arousing, here is another passage:

> *"If a man lies with a man as one lies with a woman, both of them have done what is detestable. They must be put to death."*
> —Leviticus 20:13

This is not homophobic. It's homo-cidal.

Okay. Sexual fire quenched. Let's move on.

RIGHT THERE! Sex is like the death penalty: one outcome, so many different ways of carrying it out.

STRAIGHT TALK: Even though both men and women enjoy sex, they approach it very differently. Let's be honest. Men think about sex non-stop, and that's not just a stereotype. It happens on sitcoms and in advertisements all the time.

---

[2] *If you think temporary tattoos are okay, perhaps I can interest you in some temporary eternal damnation?*

They even have a different word for it: "Love."

Women don't feel that way about sex. They prize emotion over physicality. They want a partner who is considerate and attentive, who will spoon them while reciting Keats and feed them organic yogurt by candlelight on a seaside cliff at sunset.

But here comes the Women's Studies Brigade, railing about how Colbert is reinforcing gender stereotypes. Well, ladies, we have those stereotypes for a reason—a reason I can't remember right now because I'm too busy thinking about sex more than you do. Don't be a knuckle sandwich. The sooner we accept the basic differences between men and women, the sooner we can stop arguing about it and start having sex.[3]

Pink = girl, blue = boy. (Though powder blue is a little fey.)

THE TAKE-ME-HOME: Treat sex like alcohol. Whether you sip it or chug it or have a destructive chemical dependency on it, make sure you're in control. When you bring that frosty can of sex to your lips, you'd better be the one calling the shots. One way to tell if you're losing control is if during the past three months, in order to get more sex in a shorter amount of time, you have resorted to using a funnel.

Don't become a slave to sex. Agree on a safe word.

WHEN ANIMALS ATTACK OUR MORALS

As you can see, when you follow the rules there is nothing more beautiful than two mature people who are in a committed, loving relationship doing something unspeakably debasing.

The key word there is "people," because when it comes to doing "it" right, there is no greater threat to our democratic sexual values than the Animal Kingdom. Every day, scientists report more species engaging in homosexual behavior, while cable television offers a full slate of animal sex propaganda ranging from Animal Planet to *Dora the Explorer*.

Chilling endorsement of human/ape relations

Our proud tradition of structured human courtship is under attack—the lions are circling, waiting for our children to wander away from the village so they can hump in front of them.

Odds are it's a gay pride.

---

[3] *Although sometimes there's nothing better than having sex while arguing.*

Need proof? Look no further than where animals rank on my continuum of sexual morality:

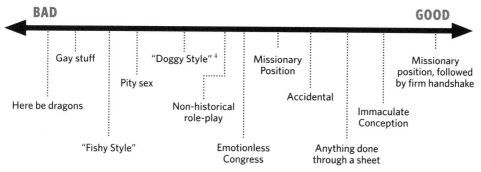

For our future's sake, Nation, I resolved to learn everything there is to know about these godless Zoodomites. Join me as I barge into Nature's bedchambers, shining the spotlight of my judgment on its bestial copulations.

BRIEF LIST OF ANIMALS THAT HAVE SEX

1. Dogs
2. Elephants
3. Spiders
4. Bears
5. Owls
6. Whales
7. Barn Owls

…and *hundreds more.*

Folks, in the Animal Kingdom, you can't turn over a rock without finding a half dozen **earthworms** doing the horizontal spermatophore, with nary a wedding ring in sight. Like we don't have enough fatherless annelids crowding our driveways and compost heaps. I don't care if you are an adult in worm years, Mr. Worm—if you can't handle tending a few thousand cocoons, don't ventrally fertilize your hermaphroditic partner.[5]

And did you know that **ants** have sex? It can't be for procreation—there are plenty of ants already. No, the simple truth is they delight in fornicating—and in plain sight of human picnics, no less. I guess that's part of the sick thrill.

Aunts also have sex.

---

[4] *Believe me, what dogs actually do is far worse than their namesake style.*
[5] *If you lost your lunch at "spermatophore," then whatever you do, don't look up "hemipenis."*

> **I VOTE "NEIGH":** Sorry horses, but the only thing I want to see mounting another horse is a jockey.

If humans should be following anyone's example, it's the **tiger**. Males and females lead chaste, solitary existences for almost their entire adult lives, until the man decides it's time to have children, spends months tracking a mate without her knowledge, then with a mighty roar leaps from the underbrush and snarls until the female performs a sexy dance. When the male is sufficiently entertained he bites her neck and initiates the miracle of life, I'm sure in a loving way. Sometimes the most beautiful, intimate connections only occur after a good, long stalking. I think it's easy for humans, especially women, to forget that. And really, ladies, when's the last time you worked on your sexy dance?

Saw this on PBS, but I didn't pledge a cent.

Unfortunately, most of today's women resemble **bowerbirds** that force suitors to build elaborate nests of twigs, leaves, and discarded garbage before choosing a mate. Any male who doesn't meet her standards doesn't get to mate that year; one assumes he just stays in his bower, reads bower manuals, and watches bowerbird porn. Hey gals, not every guy is Ryan Gosling from *The Notebook.*

Even worse is the **seahorse**. The man seahorse shoulders the burden of carrying baby seahorses to term. The seahorse is by far the most whipped animal, and by far the most frequently cited in my own marriage.

Of course, you could also be a male **octopus**, who after a lovely evening of cephalopod merriment, gently fills one of his arms with sperm before detaching said arm and watching it crawl into his life-mate's mantle cavity. Oh, don't worry, he doesn't feel a thing BECAUSE HE'S DEAD. Remember how he *detached part of his body?* It just proves that even under the sea, women will go to any length to limit a man's options. Hold on to those arms, fellas, I don't care if she has the ocean's most iridescent chromatophores.

Is this an octopus mating? Who knows?

Their "monkey business"? Peddling smut.

By far the most promiscuous animal is the **bonobo**, a species of chimpanzee that will apparently swing on any vine: girl-on-girl, guy-on-guy, something called "penis fencing." All they're missing is a sub-class of bonobo pornographers to roll tape they can sell to hard-luck bowerbirds.

Luckily, for every bonobo there's a…**New Mexico whiptail lizard!**

Wondering why you've never heard of these from the Free-Animals'-Willies crowd? Maybe it's because they don't have sex at all. They reproduce by parthenogenesis, the way God intended. It's got Genesis right there in the name. It's a travesty that these reptilian paragons of morality go sorely neglected as high school mascots, while sex fiends like Hawks, Cougars, and Wildcats get stitched onto our daughters' sweaters!

GUT CHECK: So far, you've learned everything you always wanted to know about sex that I was willing to tell you. Except one thing: how to get it. In olden days, it was simple. You just accepted her along with a large amount of gold to cement the merger of your Empires. But today it can be so complicated.

TALES FROM THE HEART:

The year: yesteryear.

The scene: a bowling alley.

I was on my first date with Tr-cy G-ll-w-y (as a gentleman, I never reveal the vowels in the names of my former conquests).[6] She was a dark-haired beauty I had met the previous Sunday at a fraternity mixer. Back then, I was shy, and it had taken me all night to work up the courage to send a letter to her parents requesting their permission to take her out. Lucky for me, they had returned it with the "yes" box checked. So here I was, watching lovely Tr-cy approach the lane with a determined stride. Needless to say, I crushed her, 134 to 62. Women respond to dominance, and when I got that tenth frame spare, I knew I had sealed the deal.

I got to th-rd b-s-.

> **MY TURN:** I've had hundreds of girlfriends.

---

[6] *Tr-cy G-ll-w-y is actually a composite of several girls I dated, including Tracy McGee and Evie Galloway.*

Growing up, I lived in a strict household. All I knew of the opposite sex was what I read on my mom's shampoo bottles. Women cared about smelling terrific, and they liked to be made to feel soft, silky, and very shiny. While other kids started "petting" and "going down to petting town" as early as sophomore year, I was a late bloomer. But I don't regret it, because once I bloomed, I turned out to be just what women love: a sex flower.

I have received many compliments on my stamen.

I'll admit it: I miss my swinging bachelor days. I used to have dating down to a science. But now that I've permanently and happily hung up my single-guy sombrero, I'm glad to share my trade secrets with the next generation.

It's on a hook in my attic.

FOR THE LADIES

Dating Do's

First, some crucial advice: **Be on your guard.** You might be looking for a life partner, but your date's most likely looking for a disco partner. Being cautious lets a man know that he'll have to put in some effort to make your acquaintance, and the right kind of guy will respect you for it. That said, **show some cleavage.** It lets a man know that you're confident enough to show some cleavage. So put on something that makes you feel like he'll feel you're sexy, and get ready to have fun. If you go out to dinner, **let him pay.** You deserve it. Plus, offering to pay makes you look like you've got money to burn. Before you know it, he'll be hitting you up for loans and asking to borrow your car. I've done it dozens of times. And during the meal, **order something that will get his attention**, like a side of bacon for dessert. I can't think of anything sexier.

Except maybe Canadian bacon. Exotic.

FOR THE FELLAS

How to entice a woman

Real ladies want a Real Man. What's a Real Man? Well, I'm a Real Man, and there's nothing I can do about that, even though some people want me to apologize for it. Well, no go. I will continue treating a lady like a lady even though it's enough to get you smacked with a lawsuit these days. My legal defense team has advised me not to say more about it than that.

So, what is a Real Man, again?

A Real Man is someone who walks through life the way a pilot walks through an airplane. Cool, calm, and checking out the sexy stews. No matter how tough the situation gets, a Real Man never lets on about the faulty landing gear.

They'll find out soon enough.

The point is, if you want to attract the ladies, there are a few things you will need to know about being a man, and luckily for you, you've come to the right book.

How to tie a bowtie

Let's face it—ladies like a man who looks good, and part of this means dressing well. In my line of work, I'm in a tuxedo all the time. It's the Emmys one week, announcing a boxing match the next. But even if you're a garbage man or you work at MSNBC, you're going to want to know how to tie a bowtie. Clip-ons are for losers. Nothing ruins your special date night faster than having someone come up to you and say, "Can we get some more shrimp puffs?"

So here's how you do it…

Start with the left end a little longer than the right end. That's *your* left. If someone else is tying it on you, it's their *right*. If you're left-handed, you're on your own. Now, slip the short end under the long end. After that, slip the long end under the short end.[7] Now, fold the short end into a bow shape and, holding that against your neck, fold the long flap over the front of the tie. There should be a little pocket in there. Push the rest of the tie through that. Goddamn it! That does not look right. Take that part of the tie out. Pinch it a little and feed it through there until it looks nice. Smooth out the right side. Slip a finger into the left bow. Pull the left bow through the hole. Great, it's all jumbled. Try holding on to the right side. Man, this looks like shit. Let's start again.

Okay, grab the three layers on the right and gently pull the left bow through the hole. Flatten the left half of the front. That'll have to do.

Hint: Buy an ascot.

How to act in the Men's locker room

This really doesn't have anything to do with dating, but hey, as a man it's something you should know. The gym is a minefield of homo-danger. So watch your eyes. I recommend focusing on the lockers themselves. Examine the metal

The towel-snapping alone

---

[7] *That's what she said!!!*

ventilation grooves and how the latch engages with the lock. One misplaced look can lead to all sorts of unpleasant misunderstandings. We've all been there. One minute you're toweling off your shins, next moment you're at a nightclub named "The Gandy Dancer" toweling off everything else.

How to ask out a woman

98% of the confusion in modern relationships starts right here. Be direct about your intentions, like this: "Good evening, (Insert Girl Name Here), would you be interested in going on a date and potentially bearing my children and quitting your job to raise them?" They'll appreciate your candor. Don't fall into the trap of saying something like "Hey, how would you like to hang out sometime?" Then the girl doesn't know if it's a date or not. And one thing leads to another and the next thing you know you're living with a woman who might just be your friend.

Flipside? She'll go halfsies.

How to act on the first date

If you want your first date to lead to another, follow these two simple rules. One, ALWAYS order for the woman. She's wrapped up in food issues. A woman is afraid if she orders the entrée she's going to look like a pig, but if she only gets a salad, you'll think she's anorexic. Take the guilt and shame away from her. Plus, it lets her know who's going to be in charge in the bedroom. Two, don't do all the talking. It's rude. Do two-thirds of the talking. That's why I keep a chess clock in my jacket pocket.

Lower your expectations

A date doesn't have to be perfect. You're not going to the barber, for goshsakes. Are you about to meet the woman of your dreams? Probably not. So just think of each date as a love scrimmage to prepare you for the marriage playoffs. Nobody's keeping score. But for the record, I'm winning.

Be a gentleman

Chivalry never goes out of style. Open doors; pull out chairs; offer to undo your own belt.

How to dance

No way around it, women will judge your potential in the sack by how you acquit yourself on the dance floor. So, a few rules. Never dance alone. If you have to, hover-dance around the perimeter of a group of women dancing together and wait for one to respond to your display. Try holding your arms akimbo. In the poor lighting of a dance club, this makes you appear larger. If one of them does turn to you, *apply your move.* I do what I call the "Colbert Shuffle." I shuffle to the left for four steps, then shuffle back to the right for four steps. Adjust to tempo.

Pointing and laughing is a response.

THE COLBERT SHUFFLE

STEP 1

2 1 4 3 6 5 8 7
7 8 5 6 3 4 1 2
L R L R L R L R

STEP 2

FINDING THAT SPECIAL SOMEONE

Let face it: Finding Mr./Miss Right is no picnic.

Have you tried looking at a picnic?

But where others see a problem, I see a free-market opportunity. That's why I've set up my own dating service for the Colbert Nation. I call it ColbertCoupling. It's a great way for like-minded heroes like you to meet one another, and it should be up and running at the ColbertNation.com website by the time you read this. *[Editors note: Due to a class action lawsuit, this web service is no longer available.]*

My single friends say they're frustrated with popular dating sites like eHarmony and Match.com. No matter how much they lie on their questionnaires, they can't find that special someone. The problem is that too many of these sites rely on touchy-feely "emotional compatibility," when really all that matters is that you agree on most things. And if you're reading this, you do agree on most things, which are the things I agree on, so you've got a head start.

Here's a sample of the questionnaire potential lovebirds will encounter at my web portal. Why not stop by and give it a shot? (Especially if you're a lady. Honestly, it's kind of a sausage-fest at the moment.)

Name:

First:		Last:	
○ M.D.	○ Esq.	○ D.F.A.	○ The Damned

Check One:

○ a. Male seeking Female	○ b. Female seeking Male
○ c. Other (seeking Eternal Hellfire)	

Body Shape:

○ a. Apple	○ b. Pear	○ c. Starfruit	○ d. Human

Political leaning:

○ a. Republican	○ b. Libertarian	○ c. Republitarian	○ d. Right-leaning Liberpublican
○ e. Conservative	○ f. Conservacanitive	○ g. Republiservative	○ h. Independent (Republican)

Religion:

○ a. Catholic	○ b. Other				

George W. Bush:

○ a. Great President	○ b. Greatest President		

Highest level of education:

○ a. High School	○ b. Your old man's belt	○ c. Liberty University	○ d. There's a letter after "c"?

Marital Status:

○ a. Single	○ b. Flying solo	○ c. Alone	○ d. …so alone…

Favorite *Colbert Report* Episode:

○ a. #1013	○ b. #1144	○ c. #2087	○ d. #3011

Favorite friend from *Fox and Friends*:

○ a. Steve Doocy
○ b. Brown haired guy who isn't Steve Doocy
○ c. Whichever blonde lady they have now

Looks are...

○ a. important to me

○ b. very important to me

○ c. just plain empirically important

○ d. not important to me (blind from birth.)

I tend to think...

| ○ a. outside the box | ○ b. inside the box | ○ c. directly on the box | ○ d. near a box |

I tend to see the glass as...

| ○ a. half empty | ○ b. half full | ○ c. a handy weapon in a bar fight |

My goals in the bedroom:

| ○ a. Be fruitful | ○ b. Multiply | | |

If I assassinated any president, it would have been...

| ○ a. McKinley | ○ b. Garfield | ○ c. Lincoln | ○ d. Martin Sheen |

How satisfied am I with my looks?

| ○ a. Very | ○ b. Smugly | |

What would I do for love?

| ○ a. Anything | ○ b. Not that | |

If I were a character in an Ayn Rand novel, I'd be...

| ○ a. Howard Roark | ○ b. Ellsworth Tooey | ○ c. The guy from *Anthem* | ○ d. A total jerk |

If I were a member of the Supreme Court, and a tree, and a dessert topping, I'd be...

| ○ a. Samuel Alito / Oak / Hot Fudge | ○ b. John Roberts /Ash / Butterscotch |
| ○ c. Steven Breyer / Pine / Chocolate Jimmies | ○ d. Clarence Thomas / Sycamore / Antonin Scalia |

Mouth capacity:

| ○ a. Five eggs | ○ b. Twelve marshmallows | ○ c. Ten ping-pong balls |
| ○ d. Fist | ○ e. 16 fl. oz. (jaw wired shut) | |

If I came across a tortoise lying on its back in the desert, I would:

○ a. Flip it over and carry it to safety

○ b. Hit it with a hockey stick and see how far it slides

○ c. Spin it in place and see how long it spins

○ d. Deny that I am an android

My high school yearbook voted me Most ____ :

○ a. Single	○ b. Likely to Snap	○ c. Teachers Dated	○ d. Uncategorizable

When I'm really feeling blue, I:

○ a. Write poetry

○ b. Take a walk in the park

○ c. Drag TV under the covers and watch DVDs in my bed fort

○ d. Make everyone within reach as miserable as me

From the list of life skills below, choose the three things that you do best:

○ Negotiating business transactions	○ Missionary work
○ Raising/Caring for Children	○ Suppressing votes
○ Pleasuring my partner	○ Gospel puppetry
○ Remaining "Chertoff-like" during a crisis	○ Communicating my thoughts and feelings (about immigrants)
○ Scrapbooking	○ Making the trains run on time
○ Blocking abortion clinics	○ Being a good friend/ narc
○ Car Maintenance and Repair	○ Community Service—voluntary
○ Union busting	○ Community service—court ordered
○ Shopping	○ I am double-jointed
○ Home Shopping	○ Questionnaire-filling

Anything else you'd like to add?

○ a. No	○ b. Yes, but you've given me no space to do so

Key:

0-25 points – Passionate	25-73 points – Red Hot Lover
74-85 points – Cold Fish	86-100 points – Human Piñata

THE LOVE OF LAST RESORT

Of course, while you're beating the bushes for a mate, the answer might be to just shake the family tree. An attractive cousin might fall out.[8]

Now, Nation, I have always been pro-cousin marriage. It is a great way to keep the bloodline pure. My own family tree is not so much a tree as it is a circle. Kind of looks like a tree eating itself.

And there's nothing wrong with it.

Don't believe me? Let's ask God. He's got some hard and fast rules in this area.

Let's see…Leviticus Chapter 18 Verse 12 – *"Thou shalt not uncover the naked-ness of thy father's sister"*…blah blah blah *"thy mother's sister"*…yeech…*"of thy father's brother"*…man there were some sick Levites…*"of thy daughter-in-law"*…fair enough…*"of thy brother's wife."* Nope! Nothing about cousins.

This is great news, because dating your cousin is only a few nucleotides away from dating yourself. And I don't know about you, but I rarely get through the morning shave without wanting to ask myself out. Will I say yes? Who knows? I've yet to get up the courage.

> **YOU CAN'T HURRY LOVE**—but you can certainly take the shortcut. Instead of paging through Match.com, try flipping through the family photo album.

Did you know that the U.S. is the only Western country with cousin-marriage restrictions? Hey Congress, stay out of our bedrooms! Unless, of course, those bedrooms are filled with gay people.

Gay cousins? Tough call.

---

[8] *Hope he doesn't fall too far. Hemophiliacs bruise easily.*

CANARY IN A COAL MINE

I hope that the Heroes out there heed my advice and find the love they deserve, because there are a lot of people who don't want men and women to get together. They'd rather see us in constant battle, a war between the sexes, where the battleground is sex itself.

Case in point: Kegels.

Now, if you're like me, when you hear the word "Kegel" you immediately think of the German word for ten-pin bowling, or *kegeln*. Well, the other day I was searching the Internet for news on the latest standings in the professional Kegel league and I got the shock of my life when this shocking page from the Mayo Clinic popped up:

**Kegel exercises:
How to strengthen your pelvic floor muscles.**

Now, I'm not squeamish about the female, you know, parts. But I'm not about to go into detail about what this "clinic" is suggesting women do. Suffice it to say, they must want women to work out the muscles down there for a reason of their own.

These strengthening exercises are called "kegels" and are named for Dr. Arnold M. Kegel M.D. I've heard of some weird fetishes, but this guy must have been a real sicko.

Now, the ladies who sign on and install a Bowflex™ in their privates say that there are all sorts of benefits, including increased sexual pleasure for both partners. I'm not buying it. Hey, everyone loves a firm handshake, but who wants to buy a car from the salesman who crushes your hand in a death grip?

The worst part is that their operation is covert. Any woman could be doing it at any time, any place. Look around you right now. Do you see a woman? Is she flexing? There's no legal way to know.

What the hell are they training for? *It ain't pickin' stawberries.*

And they got us where they want us. Might as well put a bear trap in a honey pot.

So fellas, you've been warned. From here on out, every casual conquest has been turned into a deadly game of vaginal roulette.

Wow, "vaginal roulette." That was a little racy. I'm out of breath, and I'm sure so are some of you. Let's take a cool shower in Matthew 5:29—*"If your eye —even if it is your good eye—causes you to lust, gouge it out and throw it away."*

I feel better already.

 # STEPHEN SPEAKS FOR ME
A CHANCE FOR AVERAGE AMERICANS TO AGREE WITH WHAT I THINK

Your Soul Mate

Hey there. I'm your soul mate, the one person on this earth who's perfect for you in every way. Yes, I exist, and yes, everyone else you've been with is a pale substitute. We're meant to be together, but we've never met.

You see, there are 6 billion people in the world and you encounter at most about 1,000 people per day, so statistically our paths would cross only once every 16,500 years. If we're going to beat those odds you need to work harder, because so far you've done a spectacular job of messing this up.

Remember when you bought that pack of gum and the clerk asked if you wanted a bag, but you were in a rush so you said no? If you'd waited that extra three seconds you would have missed the next train, making you late for the play, so they wouldn't have let you in the theater until the first scene was over, and I would have entered the lobby—also late—and we'd have gotten to talking. We probably would have just skipped the play and gotten coffee and then…Pow! Fifty years of golden summers at the lake house.

Another example: Remember when you signed up for a yoga class? You should have signed up for a pottery class. I was taking a pottery class! How hard is that to figure out? And don't just sign up for a pottery class next time, because I might have moved on to hip-hop cardio. I can't tell you exactly where I'll be because if you're really my soul mate you'll just *know*. Please just get it right. Last time, I dealt with my disappointment by sleeping with the pottery instructor.

I guess what I'm saying is, next time you think about going to the museum today instead of tomorrow when I'll be there, ask yourself: Do you really want to spend the rest of your life alone? Are you going to take the bus or are you going to walk? If you do walk and it's raining, how are you going to see me under my umbrella, unless I don't have one and you share yours, or I share mine and that's how we meet? So remember: Never leave the house without an umbrella… or with one. It's your choice. I think I explained pretty clearly what's at stake.

Are you reading this at a book store? I'm right behind you. Turn around!

Am I still there?

God, you're a slow reader.

Point is, hanging over every decision you make, however small, is the sword of our loneliness. I am out there. Find me. But please hurry. I know we're meant to be together for eternity, but I can't wait forever.

Oh my God! I just ran into my pottery teacher. That's so random.

FUN  ZONE

SEXUAL ROLE-PLAY QUIZ

Keeping a relationship fresh for years after attraction has faded takes work. I'm talking about **Fantasy role-playing**. It's a time-tested sexual super-charger that allows a couple to pretend in an intimate and loving way that they are making love to someone they don't know. But just because it's naughty, doesn't mean it's a free for all. There are rules. If your spouse comes out of the bathroom wearing nothing but a red hood and a basket of goodies, you sure as hell better have a wolf head on.

Match these other sexual fantasy players from the left column with their appropriate partner on the right. Good luck!

fig 9. **STEPHEN COLBERT**

★ ★ ★

CHAPTER 7

HOMOSEXUALS

"Just wrap your legs 'round these velvet rims.
And strap your hands 'cross my engines."
–"Bruce," Rock-Hard Jersey Shore-boy

 AM A GAY AMERICAN. AND I COULDN'T BE GAYER NOW THAT THE GAYS ARE ON THE RUN. OF COURSE, I'M USING "GAY" THE WAY OUR FOUNDING FATHERS INTENDED, TO MEAN "HAPPY," BEFORE IT WAS STOLEN FROM THEM BY THE GAYS, JUST LIKE THEY STOLE THEIR TIGHTS, WIGS, AND CODPIECES.

Nation, we're at War. And we can't let the gays gain any more ground on our American language. Which is why we're going to start taking their words. First word we reclaim? "Homosexual." From now on, it's going to mean what it always should have: heterosexual. Think about it. "Homo" means "the same." And we're all born with the same sexual orientation—straight. Ask any baby. *Girl babies, drop that teat*

If you don't share my outrage about this, the homosexual agenda has already got you in its velvet grip. Want to know what its other hand is doing? Just use your imagination. You're probably picturing something pretty steamy, right? Maybe a filthy little scenario taking place in a bathroom stall of a TGIFriday's while your wife and kids unsuspectingly eat their chicken wings. And your *$8.95 for 10 wings!?* little gay fantasy just proves my point. Every single one of us fights a daily battle to suppress the insurgency raging in our loins. It's a long hard slog, and we've all had the urge to cut and run.

THINGS THAT ARE TRYING TO TURN ME GAY
and
THEIR SUCCESS ON A SCALE OF ONE TO TEN

	Gay People	4
	Throw Rugs	7
	Clive Owen	8
	Origami	2
	Dog-Whispering	6
	Baby Carrots	11

But Americans are fighters. We didn't give up in World War II against the Germans just because Nazism "felt good." The homosexual agenda is nothing more than appeasement. They are sexual Neville Chamberlains. They want us to lay down our arms and pick up rainbow-colored white flags. But we can't let them win our hearts and minds with their thighs and abs. We must crush them.

a.k.a. "Richard Chamberlains"

Now I've got nothing against gay people. I just don't like how they flaunt it. I'm perfectly fine with someone choosing to be gay, as long as he marries a woman and has kids like the rest of us. And if he has to flaunt it, there's a place for that: in the privacy of his own home. Which should be a jail cell.

*Gentrify **that!***

> **GUT-SPEAKING:** We all know that people in prison engage in homosexual acts, right? Which means that criminals are more likely to be homosexuals. So wouldn't it save us a lot of tax dollars to simply throw all gay people in prison? You know, cut out the middleman.

Hey fellas, how come no middlewoman?

WHAT IS THE PROBLEM?

The problem is, these days there are more and more positive gay role models. When did gays become people to look up to? What happened to the good ol' stereotype of the creepy guy sneaking back and forth from the bar with no windows to the movie theater that doesn't say what it's showing?

Also, the movie was never in focus.

Turn on the TV these days and it's a virtual Pride Parade of admirable homosexuals. Ellen. Melissa Etheridge. Lance Bass. All the more respectable because they have the courtesy to identify themselves, unlike the "Surprise Gays." The SG's are celebrities that act manly and tough, then years later, they "come out of the pantry," and your friends start looking at you funny for having posters of them up in your weight room. All of a sudden, no one wants to spot you.

THE UNSEEN ENEMY

As I said, this is a War, and even if we win, after it's over we'll need to find where all the "land mines" are hidden so we don't step on one and have him go off in our face.

That's why I've designed this handy flow chart that will allow you to identify the enemy from a safe distance. I've gotten a lot of interest from the Department of Defense.

START

Is he wearing a dress?

NO → Is he wearing makeup?

YES → Is he taking part in a fraternity initiation?

YES → So far not gay. Just "Greek"

NO →

Is he David Beckham?

YES

NO

YES → Is he worldly, proper, clean cut, and does he make you feel like you could leave your daughter with him while you went to the movies?

NO →

YES → So far, so straight

Does he like Margaret Cho?

YES →

NO → Does he have a mustache?

NO →

YES → Are you in

NO →

Is he currently blowing you?

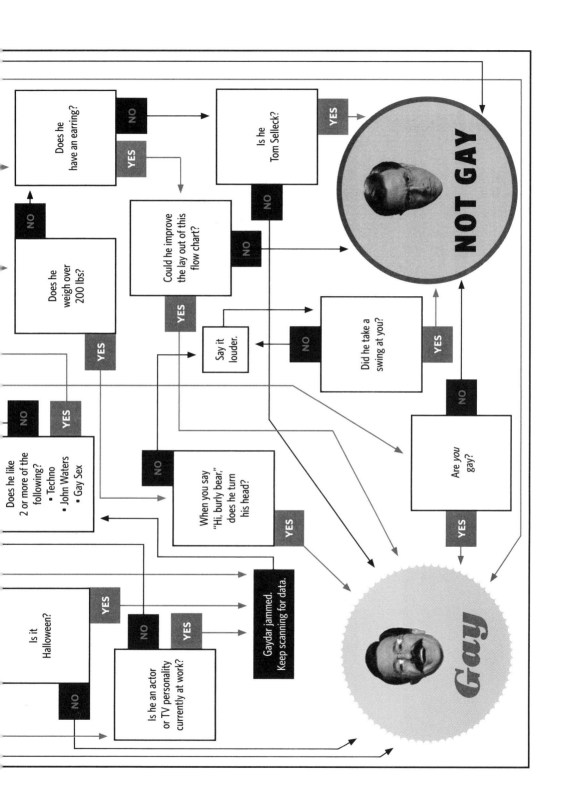

Examples of SG's are Mr. Sulu, Doogie Howser, and this one other famous guy who's about to gay surprise everybody.

It's not me.

PASTE OTHER GUY
HERE WHEN HE
GAY SURPRISES US

SO HOW DID THIS HAPPEN?

Where did all these "The Gays" come from?

Well, there are those who argue that some people are born gay. But this is just silly, because we are made in God's image. So if someone were born gay, that would mean God is part gay, and he is definitely not. He is 100% hetero. God is all Man.

And I can prove it.

BIBLICAL ACTS THAT PROVE GOD IS NOT GAY

*It's Amen—
NOT "Ah, men."*

- **CREATED MAN AND WOMAN:** Took one of Adam's ribs and made Eve. If God were gay, he would have turned Adam's rib into Dermot Mulroney.

*It's not "Hail Larry,
Full of Grace."*

- **DESTROYED THE CITY OF SODOM:** He didn't rent a summer cottage there, he destroyed it!

- **HE TURNED MOSES' "STAFF" INTO A "SERPENT":** If he was gay, it'd be the other way around.

*And it's not "Our
Father who art in
Kevin."*

- **TURNED WATER INTO WINE:** Not Appletinis. Not Cosmos. God likes his booze straight and served from an animal skin.

So I think we can put to bed this crazy idea that God is gay.

Hetero sleep

Okay, I'm gonna roust it for a second because I think it bears repeating. He's not gay. Back to sleep, idea.

And He certainly doesn't believe in Gay Marriage. The institution of marriage is meant for a man and a woman. It's right there in the Bible, right after God tells everyone to stone the gays. Nowhere does God say he wants pairs of men to be fruitful and multiply. If that's what He'd wanted, He would have given gay men ovaries and breasts and luscious lips. But he only gave them the luscious lips.

AND YET...

The biggest threat facing America today—next to socialized medicine, the Dyson vacuum cleaner, and the recumbent bicycle—is Gay Marriage.

It's like the Red Coats, Green Peace, and the Yellow Peril combined.

I call it The Lavender Armageddon. And it is the biggest threat facing America today. (See above.)

Now, the Man-Hugger huggers out there are saying, "Mary, please! What about the Iraq War? Surely that's a bigger threat than Gay Marriage." Yes, Iraq is the Central Front in the War on Terror© and We're Fighting Them Over There So We Don't Have to Fight Them Over Here.™ But consider this: who, other than terrorists, wants to destroy our way of life? The Gays. Allowing them to marry would be like strapping on a suicide vest with a matching cummerbund.[1]

They say this.

When I married my wife she became Mrs. Stephen Colbert. Likewise, I became Mr. Stephen Colbert. We went from being two autonomous individuals to a team whose sole focus was winning the game of life. By winning, of course, I mean procreation. And we have won! We have procreated. And I mean no disrespect to those readers who have not had children. There is no shame in being a genetic dead end.

Dinosaurs are extinct and more popular than ever!

Now marriage involves a lot of sacrifice. For instance, my wife frowns on me having sex with anyone but her. If marriage is suddenly available to everyone, I'm not sure I want to make those sacrifices. I guess it's like that wise old joke: I don't want to belong to any club that would have gay people as a member.[2]

At one time (I believe it was 1952), acceptance of the gay lifestyle was so low that there were exactly two homosexuals in the continental United States. One was male, and one was female, so they never tried to get married. But today tolerance is at a dangerous level, and if it keeps increasing at current rates, everyone will gay marry, and our grandchildren's grandchildren may never be born. Or worse.

They'll be gay adopted.[3]

---

[1] Yes, gays, I know: it's vest **or** cummerbund. Now do you see my point?
[2] Here's another oldie but goodie: Q: Why did the gay fireman wear red suspenders?
   A: He didn't. He **wanted** his pants to fall down.
[3] A quick word about gay children. And by that I mean "children of gays" rather than "children who are gay." I don't believe someone can choose to be gay until they've experienced either college or The Rocky Horror Picture Show, whichever comes first.

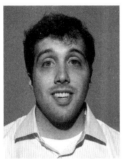

**Austin,
a formerly gay man**

My name is Austin, and I am a reformed homosexual. I was only six years old the first time I chose to pervert nature. I was with my mother at the bike store, and I decided to feel a thrill of excitement when I noticed a shiny purple Schwinn with plastic flowers on the basket.

From that point on, I chose to feel different from the other boys in my class. Until the age of twelve, I merely elected to feel a vague sense of not quite fitting in. But then, when puberty hit, I resolved to be alienated from and picked on by male peers.

I kept up this sinful pattern well into my twenties. I chose the urges that made my father stop talking to me; I selected the longings that led a group of morally stronger men to beat me up in a parking lot; I even picked the sense of contentment I felt during a three-year live-in relationship with an older man. But all that time, I knew I was living against God's will. And so, I tried everything I could think of to turn straight.

I went on dates with women. I joined a fantasy sports league. I changed the shape of my mustache.

Nothing.

I even tried hormone therapy to raise my testosterone levels. All this did was make me go fat and bald, which, in addition to my pale skin and short stature, turned me into what's known in the gay community as a "garbanzo bean." In lesbian circles they're called "chickpeas."

Then one day at Hot Yoga, I saw a flier on the Community Board about a gay rehabilitation group called God Also Yearns. They teach that God desires us to accept the true path of love.

I took the plunge and entered their proven three-part program.

- *Accept the authority of your spiritual counselors:* They not only condemned my wicked acts, but also sternly judged my clothing and income level.
- *Admit your sins:* To purge them, I wrote them down. It became a very popular blog.
- *Submit to a higher power:* This consisted mostly of electroshock.

The God Also Yearns counselors said I could be completely cured if I attended their four-week rehabilitation camp. I could only afford a two-week course. They said that would also do the trick.

They were right. At the camp, I joined in healing acts of Christian heterosexual fellowship such as heterosexual cookouts and heterosexual trust falls. The highlight of the two weeks was performing in the camp's traditional-values version of *Rent*, called *Lent*. I played Wally, the Republican Senator who casts the deciding vote for the Marriage Protection Amendment. I've never clogged with such passion.

My God Also Yearns counselors taught me that homosexuality is an addiction like smoking, only you can still do it on an airplane. To quit you have to go Cold Turkey, by imagining that your homosexual partner is a slimy, puckered, cold turkey. Unless you're into "cold turkeys," in which case you definitely need the four-week course.

Today, I am married to a wonderful woman, Afke. I don't hide my shameful past from her. During the physical act of love I will often talk about it just to remind us both how much better it is with a girl.

I also call in to a number of radio shows.

I hope my story is inspiring to any homosexuals who have bought this book not to read, but to carry as a signal to other homosexuals that they are willing to be approached and seduced. This book's distinctive cover would make it exceptionally good for that, but take it from me: there is another choice.

THE FINAL THREAT

"The greatest trick the devil ever played was
convincing the world that he did not exist."

—Charles Baudelaire, French poet, and I'm going to go out on a limb here and say "gay guy"

As gay people are increasingly integrated into society and accepted as friends and coworkers, there is a new threat looming on the horizon.

The threat that we will forget to feel threatened by them.

On this final battlefield, the greatest casualty of all may be our anger.

TAKE SOME ACTION!

There are three simple steps you can take today to maintain your anger against the gays.

* Next time you get cut off in traffic, say to yourself, "I bet that guy is gay."

* Picture your wife cheating on you with a gay guy.

* Go to the bathroom when everyone else in the house is asleep, look straight at the guy in the mirror, and whisper, "You're gay." If he nods, you will get angry.

FUN  ZONE

THE HOMOSEXUAL AGENDA

There are two things we know for sure about gays. One: they are neat and organized.
And two: they are out to destroy our society. Know thine enemy by correctly numbering
the top ten goals of the gay agenda in order of the gays' priorities.

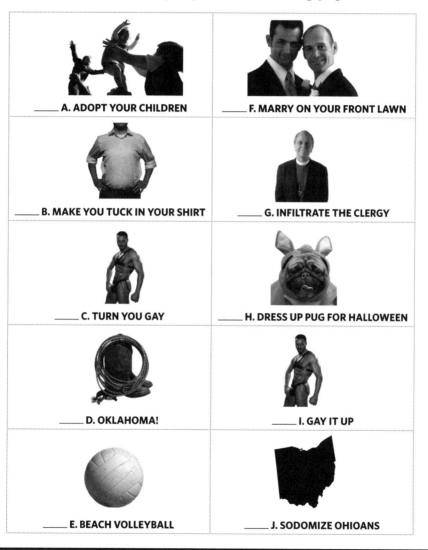

_____ A. ADOPT YOUR CHILDREN

_____ F. MARRY ON YOUR FRONT LAWN

_____ B. MAKE YOU TUCK IN YOUR SHIRT

_____ G. INFILTRATE THE CLERGY

_____ C. TURN YOU GAY

_____ H. DRESS UP PUG FOR HALLOWEEN

_____ D. OKLAHOMA!

_____ I. GAY IT UP

_____ E. BEACH VOLLEYBALL

_____ J. SODOMIZE OHIOANS

fig 10. **STEPHEN COLBERT**

CHAPTER 8

HIGHER EDUCATION

"Teach your children well."
–David Crosby, bloated folk singer
& notorious lesbian inseminator

THERE'S A BIGGER CONTRIBUTOR TO LEFT-WING ELITIST BRAINWASHING THAN COLLEGES AND UNIVERSITIES, I'D LIKE TO SEE IT. THERE'S AN OLD

Figure of speech. Don't show it to me.

SAYING, "A LITTLE KNOWLEDGE IS A DANGEROUS THING." WHICH MEANS A LOT OF KNOWLEDGE MUST BE A REALLY DANGEROUS THING. AND IT IS. LOOK NO FURTHER THAN

the example of Ted Kaczynski, a.k.a. the Unabomber. He skipped sixth grade, got a Bachelor's from Harvard followed by a Master's and a Ph.D., and then embarked on a distinguished academic career of blowing people up. Most Ph.D. biographies have similar endings.

Ted Kaczynski's last job before he went into full-time Unabombing? Assistant Professor of Mathematics at the University of California, Berkeley, a.k.a. University of Blame America First, Berkeley. Yes, folks, he capped off all those years of being a student by becoming a professor. Let's face it—he'd have been crazy <u>not</u> to go crazy, which only proves my point: the greatest threat facing America today—outside of flag burning, yoga, and vaccination—is higher education.

Hey Docs! How about a vaccine against yoga?

Just exactly what makes colleges so dangerous? It's the fact that their classrooms and lecture halls are filled with a poison known as New Ideas.

Racism, genocide, and bears were all once New Ideas.

New Ideas hurt Americans in two ways:

THE EMOTIONAL COST

Unhappy kids can skip this part.

Let me ask you this: why were you happier were when you were a kid?

Because you didn't <u>know</u> anything.

The more you know, the sadder you get.

Don't Believe Me? By the time you finish reading this chapter, over a hundred dogs and cats in animal shelters around the nation will have been euthanized.

Don't know if this is true

Bet you wish you could erase that knowledge. But it's too late. You learned a <u>New Idea</u>, and it made you sad. College is just more of the same.

THE PHYSICAL COST

Pain is the body's way of telling the brain it's in trouble. Similarly, confusion is the brain's way of telling the body, "All right, buddy, drop that book."

Let's try a little experiment. Look at this equation:

$$X = \frac{-b \pm \sqrt{b^2 - 4ac}}{2a}$$

What you're feeling right now is your body rejecting an idea that is trying to make you learn it. Don't fight the confusion. That's just your mind scabbing over in a desperate attempt to protect you from that unnatural co-mingling of numbers and letters up there. You can't add it, and you can't read it. Useless.

*Numbers **and** letters? That's a "Catch-22!"*

> **GUT-CHECK:** Son of Sam killer David Berkowitz was a well-adjusted member of society until his neighbor's dog started filling his head with a bunch of <u>New Ideas</u>.

While it's true that you encounter New Ideas in colleges and universities, they aren't the real problem. Some of the buildings are nice, and the lawns are quite lush. It's what infests these hives of higher learning that is the source of the real poison.

Writing fans: Watch for this bee metaphor to reappear later!

I'm talking about Academics.

Not a day goes by without a news of **some** anti-American statement made by a lunatic in a mortar board and elbow patches.

> **HERE'S A QUESTION:** Elbow patches? Just what are these lecherous lecturers doing behind their lecterns that wears out their elbows so fast? I've got twenty-year-old suits, and the elbows are pristine.

Why can't we fire these "edu-bators"? These men and (all too frequently) women who actually give *credit* for learning a foreign language? Because of a little thing called tenure. Well, I have a modest proposal for changing all that. Doctors don't get tenure. Plumbers don't. Can you imagine if baseball players got tenure, and we had to sit there watching them round the bases in a wheelchair?

"edu-bator"
©Stephen Colbert
2007

I can imagine this.

I propose that we do away with tenure on campus once and for all and replace it with a series of clear-cut requirements for professors. In no particular order:

Actually, in this particular order.

- **Cognitive skills test:** Prospective faculty can demonstrate mental competence by memorizing a small passage of text, say, a secret loyalty oath.
- **U.S. History:** Name the winner of the 1943 World Series. I got this idea from an old World War II movie about a squadron that had been infiltrated by a spy. I can't actually answer this question myself, but I'm not the one whose patriotism is in question.

  I may have dreamt it.

- **Penmanship:** Can a professor legibly write a brief paragraph? For instance, a secret loyalty oath?
- **Eat a bug:** Prove you love your country as much as the contestants on *Fear Factor*.
- **Public speaking:** Can the faculty member enunciate the secret loyalty oath when they are called upon to do so by a tribunal?
- **Good-faith attempts at heterosexuality:** Prospective professors would be required to produce evidence of at least five years' worth of heterosexual congress. (I'm open-minded. I don't say you must be straight to teach our youth. I only ask that you try.)

It involves a glass rod and a hammer!

- **Loyalty:** If they fell into enemy hands, could the professor keep the loyalty oath secret? No matter what unspeakable act be visited upon them?
- **Essay:** Why Ayn Rand would thrash Shakespeare in a fair fight. This isn't a metaphor for the disparity in the receptions afforded their differing philosophies in today's left-leaning universities. Professors would be required to describe how she'd kick his ass in a bar.

FROM BAD TO WORDS

Told you it was coming back

The easiest way for college professor "bees" to administer their "idea poison" is through their "thought-stingers," commonly called "books."

> **WAKEUP CALL:** Think books aren't scary? Well, think about this: You can't spell "Book" without "Boo!"

The only good book is the Good Book. Come on, the word "Good" is right there in the title. And if there's one thing you can learn from the Bible, it's that books are responsible for the Fall of Man. Look at the story of Adam and Eve. Their lives were pretty great—until they ate fruit from the Tree of Knowledge.

Now, you don't have to be a biblical scholar to see that the fruit clearly represents a book. First, both come from a tree. Second, if my first point didn't convince you, I'm not going to waste my breath with another.

God's point: Ignorance isn't just bliss, it's Paradise.

Unfortunately, Paradise is Lost, and Ignorance may no longer be an option. The Sad Truth is Knowledge has become a racket, and these days it's nearly impossible for the uneducated to break into the world of highly paid professionals. Doctors and lawyers (even some *dentists*) have to go college. So to live in the gated communities to which you'd like to become accustomed, you've got to play ball. College Ball.

GETTING IN

First off, if you're going to squander your youth in the Ivory Jungle, at least shoot for the Top Schools. They provide something the best firms look for, called *cachet*.

Note: The "t" is silent. Classy.

Rule of Thumb: If they're not in the first two pages of *U.S. News and World Report College Guide,* all they offer is information and the possibility of drunken sex with your suitemate—a dangerous potential that will gnaw at you for the rest of your life.

Did your suitemate gnaw on you?

The ultimate goal of going to a Top School is the quiet satisfaction of whipping out your Alma Mater at opportune moments. At first blush, most would peg me as an average Joe, and I'm proud of that. But my sheepskin announces to all assembled that though I may be a man of the people, I also have the keys to the clubhouse. I can't count the number of times I've heard the phrase, "You went to Dartmouth? I find that hard to believe."

Heard it while at Dartmouth, too

THE BAD NEWS

Admissions is an arbitrary and demoralizing process, and no matter how hard you work, the outcome is often determined by personal connections. You know what else is like that?

Life.

Also, love-tester machines. No way I'm a "Cold Fish."

I'm at least a "Pretty Spicy."

THE GOOD NEWS

There's an entire industry in this country devoted to getting kids into college.

And while you may not need Kaplan's or *The Princeton Review* to get into a decent school, you should pay for them anyway. We live in a capitalist society. Love it or leave it.

Applying to college teaches youngsters résumé-building, a.k.a.: lying. Here's how it works, kids. Let's say one day you're bored in class, so to pass the time, you make out with the Danish exchange student across the aisle. Now, on your college application, you can say that you carried out an Independent Study in Foreign Tongues.

"Hands" Christian Andersen

I went to Dartmouth.

BY THE NUMBERS: Even the least-padded résumé can be overcome with a solid application essay. Here's the one that got me into Dartmouth:

"America is therefore the land of the future, where in the ages that lie before us, the burden of the World's History shall reveal itself," said the philosopher, scholar, and lover-of-thought George Wilhelm Friedrich Hegel.

This tract reminds me of the egregious hardships and unwelcome adversity I faced last summer, when I toiled laboriously on my grandfather's venison farm. It was my duty and task to deal the hinds a deadly coup de grace rifle blow at close range while they grazed luxuriously upon the surrounding foliage. Often, I would summon the impoverished and penurious children who lived adjacent to my grandsire's acreage to assist me with my encumberage, thus imparting to them the sublime significance of firearms. Recieving these pauperized youngsters unto my tutelage was the apex, pinnacle, acme, vertex, and zenith of my life's experience.

In conclusion, my great-great-uncle was Daniel B. Fayerweather of Fayerweather Hall.

There are two secrets that make this essay great.

Secret number one: A Thesaurus. Eggheads love the words, so the more you jam in there, the better. Think of it as a verb sausage.

Secret number two: The last sentence. All it takes is a little research, and you can find the campus library, dormitory, or stadium that most plausibly could have been donated by your family. You'd be surprised how rarely these folks check into your background if you show up to the interview wearing an ascot.

CHASE CUTTING: You got in! Feel good? It should. You were deemed worthy, while your high school rival is going to his safety school.

Baghdad State

NOW WHAT?

When you get to college you'll be on your own, maybe for the first time in your life. You will soon learn that peer pressure is a terrible thing. You're going to be tempted to go follow the crowd—into a classroom. Fight it. Because there's no need to attend a single lecture.

Don't believe me? Professor Colbert is going to tell you all you need to know.

You're about to get four years' worth of college in five minutes. I went through the course catalogue for a prestigious university—I won't say which, because I might have a shot at an honorary doctorate there—and I found that I could reduce the pertinent content of every class into one sentence. I didn't include graduate classes, because if you're even considering an advanced degree, I've already lost you.

C LIT 211	LITERATURE AND CULTURE NEITHER ONE WILL PROTECT YOU FROM A TERROR ATTACK. PLUS, C LIT IS NOT WHAT YOU THINK.
C LIT 314	THE NORTHERN EUROPEAN BALLAD HEY NONNY, NONNY, WHO GIVES A CRAP?
C LIT 342	LITERATURE OF PACIFIC ISLANDERS BEWARE. THERE'S A LOT MORE LITERATURE BY PACIFIC ISLANDERS THAN YOU'D THINK
CSE 322	INTRODUCTION TO FORMAL MODELS IN COMPUTER SCIENCE SOME PEOPLE JUST DON'T LOSE THEIR VIRGINITY, EVER.
DANCE 306	DANCE FOR MEN GO AHEAD. BREAK YOUR MOTHER'S HEART.
DRAMA 101	INTRODUCTION TO THE THEATRE SOME LUCKY STUDENT IS GOING TO SLEEP WITH THE PROFESSOR. IT COULD BE YOU!
ENG 324	CAREERS IN POETRY JUST MOVE BACK IN WITH YOUR PARENTS NOW.
ETHN 384	INTERRACIAL DYNAMICS BETWEEN WOMEN OF COLOR IT'S NOT WHAT YOU THINK.
H ART 331	NATIVE ART OF THE PACIFIC NORTHWEST COAST OOH, LOOK. SOMEBODY DREW A SALMON!
PHIL 101	INTRODUCTION TO PHILOSOPHY IF A TREE FALLS IN THE FOREST AND NO ONE HEAR IT, I HOPE IT LANDS ON A PHILOSOPHY PROFESSOR
PHIL 356	INTRODUCTION TO METAPHYSICS NOTHING HERE YOU CAN'T PICK UP BY EATING THE WRONG MUSHROOMS ON A CAMPING TRIP.
PSYCH 101	INTRODUCTION TO PSYCHOLOGY SO THEY MADE YOU USE A TOILET. GET OVER IT.
REL 212	COMPARATIVE RELIGION JESUS WINS.
REL 308	INTRODUCTION TO ISLAM IF YOU TAKE THIS CLASS, THE TERRORISTS HAVE W0
SCI 252	INSECT BEHAVIOR THERE'S NO WAY I'M GETTING RID OF THOSE CARPENTER ANTS WITHOUT AN EXTERMINATOR
SOC 360	ETHNIC STEREOTYPES AND THE HUMOR OF CRUELTY A PROFESSOR WILL TELL YOU A BUNCH OF HILARIOUS JOKES, AND YOU'RE NOT ALLOWED TO LAUGH
C HIS 416	20TH CENTURY MEXICAN SOCIAL MOVEMENTS THE MOVEMENTS ARE NORTHWARD, TAKE PLACE AT NIGHT
WOMEN 357	WOMEN ON WOMEN: THE LITERATURE OF LIBERATION. IT'S NOT WHAT YOU THINK

Now you that you have your education covered, what will you do with all that free time? Well, luckily, college is good for one thing. Can you guess what it is? I'll give you a hint: it starts with "secret" and ends with "societies."

Whether they be Fraternities or Eating Clubs or (in Louisiana) Parishes, universities are the best places a young man can meet and bond with, through an elaborate hazing process, those who can give him a leg up for the rest of his life.

I cemented my lasting relationships with America's future movers and shakers by being forced to strip naked with half my fellow pledges and pass a greased 45 rpm record of Foreigner's "Hot Blooded" from ass crack to ass crack. It could have been worse. The other half of the pledges were passing a greased turntable.

Still played post-crack. Let's see an MP3 do that.

Don't believe me? While most of his peers at Yale were writing essays about the tension between stasis and dynamism in *Mariana in the Moated Grange*, young George W. Bush was making the connections that would eventually lead to him becoming the most Powerful Man in the World.™

In your face, whoever's in charge of China!

I speak, of course, of **Skull and Bones**, a shadowy organization that admits only the most deserving Yalesmen. Its members swear an oath of secrecy, and use their wealth and access to power to promote one another once they graduate into the "real world." For well over a century, Skull and Bones has provided a safe and brotherly environment where future Supreme Court Justices, Presidents, and Captains of Industry can gather to urinate on Geronimo's bones.

THE TAKEAWAY: Contrary to what you'll be taught in college, evolution is a farce, but Darwin did have one good idea: Social Darwinism. You see, in the animal kingdom, God grants long life to whichever lion He thinks is prettiest. But in the world of human society, only the strongest, boldest, and worthiest individuals have the most sex, get the most power, and live the longest. College is the place to meet those people, and once you do, find out their darkest secret.

It may come in handy some day.

It probably involves their suitemate...and some New Ideas!

STEPHEN SPEAKS FOR ME

A CHANCE FOR AVERAGE AMERICANS TO AGREE WITH WHAT I THINK

**Doctor Bernard Brunner
Distinguished Professor**

March the 13th, this two thousand and seventh year of what some may consider Our Lord.

I am Doctor Bernard Brunner, distinguished professor at a well-known and esteemed liberal arts university. Some may query, "Of what are you scholarly?" Tragically, even I am not quite certain of that which is my endeavor. It ends in –ology?

I am certain only of this—that life is fleeting and that much of my own has been wasted within the confines of small rooms and even smaller minds. I have spooled the thread of my life arguing meaningless rhetorical questions with unformed, untried brains and vainly pressing nimble, young flesh into service.

Oh, to feel the biting wind on my face. To wake in the early, still dark morn and milk a barn full of swelled cows. Or perhaps to live in the rough city, grasping steel work parts in my hard-calloused hands, the merit badge of the working man!

But alack, harsh fate has decreed that none of these paths will be mine. For I have tenure, and she is far too comforting a mistress to loose me from her grasp for long.

I lay in her arms and suck from her teat, fat and oily.

And here I sit. And here I shall sit.

And like a sneaky merman singing on the rocks, I try to lure young sailors away from the charted waters to a harsh and certain doom. Plug your ears, and though you be young, be wise! Listen not to me, and distrust me upon first sight! I will trap you in the learnings of the past. Look to the future! Away! Good sea!

You must live to learn. Pray live. Whilst I, like all unnecessary things, do but shrivel…

Dry out… And turn to dust.

With the most sincere of wishes,

Dr. Bernard Brunner, Ph.D.

FUN  ZONE

Name The Aca-demon Lurking Behind The Beard

1 Ted Kaczynski   **2** Gloria Steinem   **3** Charlie Manson   **4** Evil Spock

A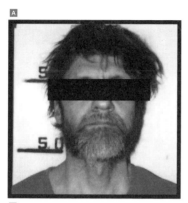

B

C

D

HINTS

1. He led a small coven of fanatical followers who called themselves "The Family." Often called the "Fifth Beatle."

2. Has led a large coven of fanatical followers who called themselves "The Lesbians." I had a three-way with her and Jane Fonda.

3. His cold logic, or "book-thinking," masks a sociopathic indifference to human emotion. Bonus Hint: he tortured the mirror-world version of Mr. Chekhov in an "agony booth" in "Mirror, Mirror" (episode #33, original airdate 10/6/67).

4. Enjoyed blowing people up through the mail.

fig 11. **STEPHEN COLBERT**

★ ★ ★

CHAPTER 9

HOLLYWOOD

"Those Hollywood nights, those Hollywood Hills."
–Bob Seger, Rocker Laureate of General Motors

NOTHING CAN MATCH THE EXHILARATION OF SETTLING INTO YOUR SEAT IN A DARK MOVIE THEATER, HEADY WITH ANTICIPATION. THE SCREEN LIGHTS UP! FINALLY, THERE IT IS: THE FIRST PRE-TRAILER ADVERTISEMENT. WILL THE HERO BE ABLE TO DODGE THE MYRIAD OBSTACLES ON HIS WAY TO THE

Pepsi machine? Will the girl-next-door fall for the arrogant pretty-boy with the substandard wireless service or the lovable goof with America's most reliable network, Verizon? That's what they call the "magic" of the big screen. Bravo!

Then the feature starts and the evening quickly turns sour. Within minutes, you find yourself ushering your children out the exit while you desperately try to explain to them that God is not Black.

I DON'T UNDERSTAND movies today. They romanticize the liberal lifestyle, cram gays into our living rooms, and make children believe it's safe to spend time with Robin Williams.

TOO FAR!

*Mrs. Doubtfire should be both **doubted** and **fired.***

Let's face it, next to hybrid vehicles, anchor babies, and heirloom tomatoes, there's nothing in America quite as corrosive as our so-called "Entertainment" Industry.

CULTURAL CORROSIVENESS PH SCALE

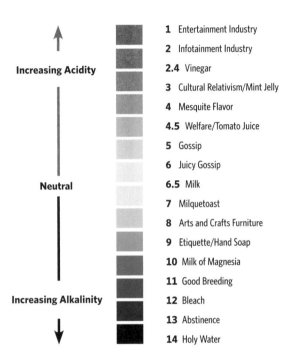

Increasing Acidity

Neutral

Increasing Alkalinity

1 Entertainment Industry
2 Infotainment Industry
2.4 Vinegar
3 Cultural Relativism/Mint Jelly
4 Mesquite Flavor
4.5 Welfare/Tomato Juice
5 Gossip
6 Juicy Gossip
6.5 Milk
7 Milquetoast
8 Arts and Crafts Furniture
9 Etiquette/Hand Soap
10 Milk of Magnesia
11 Good Breeding
12 Bleach
13 Abstinence
14 Holy Water

Don't believe me? Even my editor, Gayle, has pressured me to make this book "entertaining"! But I don't play that game.[1]

This chapter isn't going to transport you to a glamorous world of magic where wishes come true and even sociopaths like Jason Bateman can become the slam-dunking lupine beasts of their dreams.

No, this is a runaway train to Cold, Hard Realityville.

First stop, the Good Old Days, because while there's nothing more anti-American than Hollywood today, there was nothing more *All*-American than Hollywood yesterday.

[1] *Other games I don't play: Boggle, Scrabble, Scatagories, travel Yahtzee.[2]*
[2] *I will play the stationary version of Yahtzee in a vehicle, but only if the vehicle is parked and/or docked.*

NEWS ON THE MARCH!

The Time: The 1930s.

The Scene: Hollywood!

Fresh-faced hopefuls from around the nation stream to Los Angeles
with dreams of becoming the next "Steamboat Willie."

Elsewhere: Nazis!

THAT'S RIGHT: There was once a "Golden Age" of Hollywood. It was so-called because the original studio heads were the children of gold prospectors who settled in California, struck it rich, and then converted to Judaism.

Back then, movies worked. Whether they were "talkies," "soundies," or the short-lived "loudies," the films of the Golden Age had one thing in common that made them timeless classics: corporate hegemony. From the crank on the cameras to the films' shipping canisters to the dusty hat on the wrinkled old usher with the air of defeat, the "Big Five" studios owned every dimension of moviemaking. They even owned the stars.

The first film editors were moyels.

Studios would pluck promising young actors from obscurity, and with a simple name change and an ironclad lifetime contract larded with morality clauses, turn them into Hollywood legends. Actors like Joan Crawford (born Shprintzel Anatevkawitz) and Cary Grant (born Balgok-Uth, Devourer of Souls) got more than just starring roles in the hit movies of their day. They got firm moral guidance. Women could not appear in public without their makeup. Homosexual men could not appear without their "beards." Beardless heterosexual men could not appear without their "mustaches."

Exhibit A

Here's a handy chart of the Big Five studios. If you don't find it handy, try holding the book in your other hand. (See "How to Read This Book.")

THE STUDIO SYSTEM

Studio					
Early Strength	Razzmatazz	"Remarkable verisimilitude in its depiction of the appearance and customs of the fierce Indian Squaw!"	Buck-toothed manservants	Moxie	Realistic hobo bindles
Golden Age Classic	*Love Comes to Football Town* (1948)	*The Jumpy Negro* (1927)	*Rin Tin Tin Goes to Washington* (1932)	*$top That Train o' Dollar$!* (1938)	*What a Dame!* (1936)
Sign of Decline	Lion no longer devoured Japanese baby during studio title card	None. Proud subsidiary of Viacom. Keep those hits coming!	*Happy Feet* (2006). I don't want to feel any guiltier than I already do about eating penguins.	Bought by tire company.	No longer 20th century.

As you can see, for a while, everything was dandy-dory in "The City of Angels." But guess who shows up to crash the party and ruin it? You guessed it— The Supreme Court.

Did you guess it?
☐ Yes
☐ No
(Cut along line and keep in wallet)

On May 4, 1948, the Supreme Court ruled that the Big Five studios had violated U.S. antitrust laws and set off a process that led to their dissolution. Ten days later, the State of Israel was proclaimed. Coincidence?

I believe so.

ONCE AGAIN: The old adage proved true: "The Supreme Court hates America." Suddenly, it was no longer okay for studios to force their female leads to take diet pills or copulate with rams.

Ewe!

And talk about hypocrisy! In 1952, the Supreme Court made another "ruling." This time, it was that movies were protected by the First Amendment! That's right, just four years after they criminalized Hollywood's *free market*, they upheld Hollywood's *free speech*! Which is it, Supreme Court? Are "free" things good or bad?

I thought "rulings" were for kings!

Tragically, the 1952 First Amendment decision all but killed off the Production Code, the industry's guidelines for keeping movies moral. It was like the Bill of Rights, only for movies, and instead of saying what you *could* do, it said what you *couldn't*.

THE PRODUCTION CODE:
SO LONG, FAREWELL, AUFWIEDERSEHEN, GOODBYE

Cut Rolf some slack!

The Motion Picture Production Code of 1930, often called the "Hays Code" because that's what it forbade onscreen couples from rolling in, was a strict set of guidelines meant to ensure that motion pictures set a positive example. It was created to curb the corrupting influence of movies like *The Bathing Kuties of '28* and *Gangbang Dames of '29*. The Code took effect on March 31, 1930, five months too late to prevent the Wall Street Crash, but early enough to keep The Sixties from happening until approximately 1964. The Hays Code is gone now, but a look back at some of its clauses shows how much we have lost.

When America fell victim to the British Invasion

135

CODE OF CONDUCT (cont.)

657. A man and a woman must never be shown lying in the same bed, unless it has been previously established that one of them is dead.

658. Lascivious dancing shall be prohibited unless it is performed by dusky native girls. Dusky native girls shall be prohibited unless they are portrayed by white actresses.

659. Cannibalism shall not be portrayed or implied, unless hunger first drives the cannibalistic character to visualize his victim as an enormous roast chicken.

660. Seduction and rape are never proper subjects for comedy. Copping a feel shall be considered on a case-by-case basis.

661. Characters may not walk and chew gum at the same time.

662. Scenes of childbirth, in fact or in silhouette, are never to be presented. The same restriction applies to rabbits being pulled from hats.

663. If a character places a folded towel over a second character's eyes and then invites him to do a sit-up while a third character removes his pants and squats in such a manner that the sit-up will bring the second character's nose into contact with the third character's naked nether sphincter, this action must be followed by a fourth character, preferably a member of the clergy, expressing disapproval.

664. Characters must never discuss the high suicide rate among dentists in a manner that implies they "have it coming."

665. If a scene includes a train entering a tunnel, the tunnel shall not be portrayed as enjoying it.

667. Should it be necessary to the story for a character to burp, sneeze and pass gas at the same time, the action must result in death.

668. If the story calls for an animal character such as Lassie or Rin Tin Tin to save a child's life, the reward may not be "a free ride on Timmy's leg."

670. For Christ's sake, somebody put a bra on Jean Harlow.

By 1968, the Production Code was no more. But, sorry Supreme Court, its death wasn't excessive, lustful, or perverted.

Fittingly, it went out without a "bang."

> **FUN FACT:** If we still had the Hays Code, they could never have made *The DaVinci Code!*

For your moral convenience, you can use this book as an improvised Production Code.

Don't cut here

Just cut along the line and watch movies made after 1968 through the hole. Move the page around to avoid objectionable content. For instance, focus on the actors' faces, especially during sex scenes.

Be careful not to mistake Russell Crowe's ass for his face.

A WORD ON CENSORSHIP: The creative class says it's unconstitutional, but I advocate censorship. It's my First Amendment right to do so. They want you to believe censorship hinders creativity. Hogwash. Just the opposite! Take foul language. It's easy for a lazy screenwriter to put the words "fuck you, cocksucker" into a character's mouth, but the artist who translates that phrase for an airing on prime time television or a transcontinental flight is forced to come up with the much more interesting "flip you, cod bucket!" I ask you, which is more "creative"?

NEWS ON THE MARCH!

The Time: The 1950s. America loves Ike!
The scene: Washington! Cheese-fed senators from the Heartland
lead a desperate fight to keep Communist sympathizers from writing
"I Remember Mama."

Luckily, the Golden Age of Hollywood was followed by an even Goldener Age, the Age of the Blacklist. Patriotic Americans secretly denounced Hollywood's most dangerous Fellow Travellers to America's House Un-American Activities Committee, led by American hero Joe McCarthy. America.

MY TURN: One of my greatest regrets is that I never got the opportunity to "name names." And I would have named enough names to fill the Moscow phone book.

Tried without a jury

Luckily, I do have the opportunity to *rename* some names that were named all those years ago. So, here they are, a collection of blacklisted Hollywood comrades who were stopped from destroying our nation right in the nick of time. Most of the charges never added up to anything more than whispers and innuendo, but in Hollywood, whispers and innuendo are accepted as truth. If you don't believe me, ask Richard Gere's gerbil.

AMERICA-HATERS WHO WERE BROUGHT TO JUSTICE BY THE HUAC BLACKLIST

Burl Ives
Seems "Sam the Snowman" was actually "Pietrov the Pinko." Say, what color was Rudolph's nose anyway? Exactly.[3]

E.Y. "Yip" Harburg
Lyricist for *The Wizard of Oz*. Pay no attention to the man behind the Iron Curtain. Lollipop Guild? Socialism for suckers.

Bill Melendez
He produced more than 75 "Peanuts" specials, but he forgot one: *It's Treason, Charlie Brown!*

Kim Hunter
It's a bitter pill to swallow, but Dr. Zira wasn't only an evolutionist—she was a communist. Or am I being redundant?

Larry Adler
Hard to believe that the grasping claws of the Red Menace could even reach this harmonica virtuoso. Even harder to believe there's such a phrase as "harmonica virtuoso."

David Robison
When I remember that episodes of *Bewitched* were written by a Red, I shudder to think how close I came to naming my son Uncle Arthur.

Judy Holliday
"Bells Are Ringing?" Yes, Ms. Holiday. It's Joe McCarthy. He'd like to ask you a few questions. He wasn't "Born Yesterday!"

Bill Scott
Is it really a surprise that the voice of Mr. Peabody was a Commie? Or is there some *other* political system that lets dogs keep humans as pets?

---

[3] I don't want to be too hard on Burl. He eventually came around and testified to HUAC, turning in Pete Seeger. "If I Had A Hammer"...and sickle!

NEWS ON THE MARCH!

The Time: Who knows, dude?
The scene: Anywhere Far-out! Drugged-out hippies take over
the movie business. It's a bad trip, man!

Like any great era, the glorious days of the Blacklist had to end, but instead of spawning a new, Goldenest Age, Hollywood handed the keys to the kingdom to a generation of director-rebels fresh from Film School.

Once again, Higher Education took a perfectly decent slice of Americana, threw it to the ground and had its way. (Read Chapter 8 – at your own risk!)

Your Scorseses, your Coppolas, and a few non-Italian directors turned Hollywood on its ear in the name of a gritty, "realistic" style of filmmaking.[4] Movies, once fantastic dreamscapes where cowboys fought Indians and gay men kissed Elizabeth Taylor, became squalid nightmares where cowboys turned tricks and hillbillies kissed Ned Beatty.

Tip 10%
(unless they cut your
steak into tiny pieces
for you)

These new Frank *Crap*ras wanted to be "important." To regular folks like you and me, "important" is remembering to tip before tax and not putting tin foil in the microwave. To Hollywood, "important" means picking an issue no one cares about and making it a movie. Well, guess what? The Golden Age of movies tackled their fair share of "difficult issues." I can think of several memorable films that tackled the difficult issue of how to get a large number of women to fall into a pool like dominos.

Just because these days a few Hollywood elites decide some issue is "important" enough to make a movie out of, why do I have to suffer through *Syriana*? Hey George "Looney," last time I checked it was called Syria.

Full disclosure:
I have never checked.

Here's a Fact of Life. Your best work is behind you.

What went wrong?

---

[4] *I give these new movies two thumbs up—to gouge out my eyes.*

I say, if Hollywood absolutely must make a Message Movie, make one like *Starship Troopers*. This was the perfect political allegory, because I didn't get it. People tell me it was about something, but all I know is that good-guy-army-guy shot bad-guy-monster-bugs with lasers in space. Four stars!

> **AUTHOR! AUTHOR!:** The Hollywood agenda is so insidious and corrosive that I considered not devoting a chapter to it, just to be safe. I was going to fold it into the chapter on the gays or the chapter on the gay communists. [Note to Ed.—if we cut "Hunting and Mounting the American Commusexual," I walk.]

There is another dark side to Hollywood. It's not just the shattered dreams, or the cheap porn, or the moderately priced porn. There's something much worse.

That's right. Both sides are dark.

HOLLYWOOD LIBERALS

That shining city that only cares about money has an underbelly that only cares about saving the world. It's getting so America can't ignore the tiniest humanitarian crisis without some big movie star going on *Access Hollywood* to bitch about it.

I guess the Motion Picture Academy mails out a pet cause with every Oscar nomination, because no sooner do we inform a star that we like him/her than they're up on some soapbox.

But not a he/she!

You know who I'm talking about:

THE FOUR HORSEMEN OF THE APOCA-LEFT

| Sean Penn | Barbra Streisand | Tim Robbins | Kirsten Dunst |

These four are constantly whining about injustice, chaining themselves to redwoods, bad-mouthing our president, and tormenting us with their portrayals of the perfect yet unattainable hometown girl.

Somewhere along the line, these A-list A-holes confused "box office" with "running for office." **Hey Celebrities!** Just because 20 million people went to see your movie, that doesn't mean 20 million people care about your opinions! Your job is to distract us from the horrors of the world, not to call our attention to them! We just want to be entertained. We want you to make us laugh, or cry, or worry if two cheerleaders from such different backgrounds can ever bridge their differences. That's it.

They can!

And you know what? Cut it out with the fundraisers already. Who's getting all that cash? Refugees? Rain forests? Harp seals? If a Harp seal needs money that badly, it should do what I do. I hold a little fundraiser every day. It's called Going to Work. Without it, I'd be a charity case. Maybe they should give it a shot. Check the want ads—there's plenty of them out there. And don't give me "Harp seals can't survive in an office habitat," because that excuse doesn't hold water anymore, thank you very much, Americans with Disabilities Act.

Air Bud?
I blame Title IX

I'm no fan!

You Hollywood liberal elites need to realize that you wouldn't be famous at all if it weren't for Middle America. So stop trying to use your fascinating portrayals of Marie Antoinette to turn red states blue.

You have a choice. You don't have to support America—it's a free country. But if you're not going to stand up for This Land of Ours, at least be consumed by some inner demons. Snort glue. Make a sex tape. Spiral out of control in a headline-grabbing way until you're wandering toothless through Malibu backyards or telling Larry King that you speak in a musical birdlike tongue to the alien beings that visit you at night in the form of vibrating bands of color on your bedroom wall. This is very entertaining while also being a cautionary tale for our children.

So now that you know what's wrong with Hollywood, let me ask you a Question. If someone screwed off the top of your head, scooped out your brain and filled your skull with garbage, would you fight back? You bet your screw-top head you would.

Get a childproof cap on that skull!

IT'S A CULTURE WAR—TIME TO STRIKE BACK!

Unlike Paul Newman, who seems to think that salad dressing is the cure-all for America's ills, I'm a man of action. Here are a few simple steps you can take to end the stranglehold that the Entertainment industry has on our need for being entertained.

Apply Liberally

Boycott! Cut them off from your money. But just as importantly, cut their message off from your eyes. Immediately stop consuming all entertainment. This means TV, radio, movies, music, video games, magazines, newspapers, books, cell phone ringtones, the backs of cereal boxes, Bazooka Joe wrappers, riddles on Dixie Cups, fortune cookies, novelty t-shirts, and seafood restaurant placemats. Boredom will be your greatest enemy, so make your own fun. Time was a family could get a wonderful evening out of some sheet music and an egg timer. Bonus: You'll be an empty-nester years earlier than your friends.

Switch to Christian entertainment! For every corrupt Hollywood influence there's a life-affirming Christian equivalent. For instance, instead of rotting my mind with the mindless violence of a game like "Grand Theft Auto," I play "Left Behind: Eternal Forces." That way, I know every enemy I kill goes directly to Hell.

Write letters! Let the child-poisoners know that you're keeping an eye on them. Write them e-mails on an hourly basis to tell them how offensive you find the movies you're not seeing. It's amazing how easy it is to make "I'm praying for you" sound like a threat.

I'm praying for you.

Go camping! Drop off the grid and get away from the corroding influences of the debased culture and return to nature, preferably to Idaho with a group of like-minded patriots, their child brides, and a cache of weapons. You never know when Alcohol, Tobacco and Firearms is going to show up and try to make you watch *Capote*.

*Truman?
More like False-man!*

If all else fails pull the old switcheroo and:

Consume everything! Totally immerse yourself in the filth of pop culture to build a callus on your soul. It's like when my Dad caught me with cigarettes when I was twelve and forced me to finish an entire carton of Kools. Worked like a charm. Haven't smoked a menthol since.

CANARY IN A COAL MINE

If you don't think Hollywood has tricks up its sleeve, maybe you should get out of the sleeve-checking business.

The problem with Hollywood, as if there weren't enough problems already, is that the minute you've whacked that weed in one place, up it sprouts somewhere else.[5] Well, the latest rock it's crawled out from under is a doozy.

Not content to pour their poison across the silver screen, the LA studio heavyweights who run Broadway are now evidently shipping it directly to the Heartland.

Need proof? Just look at this headline out of Wisconsin from the *Appleton News-Leader:*

Disney's "The Lion King" is about to hit town

The staff of the Sommers Center for the Performing Arts is preparing for the arrival of the Broadway hit. "Everybody is very excited," said town manager Barbara Kingholm.

Sadly these milk-fed innocents clearly don't know what they're in for.

---

144 ⁵ *I recommend RoundUp by the good folks at Monsanto!*

But I've been there, so let me warn you. The effects of live theater are way harder to shake off than movies. It's frighteningly intimate and, worst of all, you've got *no control*. It's like breaking up with a girl in person.

When I watch *The Lion King* at home, I can safely end the movie before Mufasa's untimely death. But when I bring my remote control to the live performance, it doesn't work.[6] All I can do is watch helplessly as the hyenas execute their perfect crime.

"Slow down, you wildebeests! That lion is your king!"

Apparently yelling at the stage is *verboten*, even if to challenge Scar to pistols at dawn.

Because I am always ushered out at this point, but not soon enough to spare me a harsh dose of reality. You see, a movie you can dismiss when the lights come up.

But a play? *Those animals were <u>real people.</u>*

Makeup Wizardry!

**Mort Sinclair,
Former TV Comedy
Writer, Communist**

Here's a joke for you:

A man walks into a bar. The bartender says, "What will it be, Mac?" The man looks at the drink menu and says, "How 'bout a revolution of the proletariat?"

Zing! I wrote that one for Dinah Shore back in 1954.

You see, I used to be a comedy writer, and like many comedians during the '50s, there was nothing I wanted more than to use my jokes to overthrow the government and replace it with a classless Communist society.

It all started when I was a kid. I remember sitting in the movie house watching The Three Stooges, hearing everyone laugh, and thinking to myself, "I know what I want to do. Undermine the capitalist system and replace it with collective farms."

Quick! A man and his wife are lying in bed. The wife says, "Honey, why don't you roll over here and kiss me?" The man says, "I would, but I'm shackled by my capitalist oppressors!" Hot-cha!

The first job interview I had was with Milton Berle. I'll never forget what he said to me after reading my joke packet: "Good material, kid, but I think you can inject more references to the industrial class structure."

And he was right. Only three of my jokes mentioned the evils of private ownership. That's comedy gold! To me the perfect joke didn't end with a laugh, but with an agonizing reappraisal of the worker's suppression by the entrenched plutocrats.

It's funny because it's true.

Of course, my career as a TV comedy writer wasn't always easy. But whenever things got rough, I'd remind myself that if my jokes got just one person to sell nuclear secrets to the Russians, then it was all worth it.

I'll leave you with this joke I wrote for Sid Caesar:

"President Truman is like Communist ideology. No class."

Za-bang!

FUN  ZONE

Match the Celebrity with Their Pet Cause

1 Leonardo DiCaprio

2 Rosie O'Donnell

3 Sheryl Crow

4 Alec Baldwin

A "End the war in the Middle East!"   **B** "Equal rights for homosexuals!"

C "Stop global warming!"   **D** "Hey! Look at me!"

Part Three

MY AMERICAN MATURITY

★ ★ ★

In 1997, I was made the anchor of the Channel 7 News on WPTS Patterson Springs, North Carolina. I got promoted after I narced out the previous anchor, Wayne Colt, for his coke addiction and won a local Emmy for my investigative report, "Anchor Away: The Tragic Downward Spiral of Wayne Colt."

I was getting too big for Patterson Springs (Pop. 620), so that fall I sent out a reel of my best reports: "From Wayne to Worse: The Continuing Struggles of Wayne Colt," "Wayne Damage: The Hidden-Camera Footage Wayne Colt Begged Me Not to Show You," "Wayne, Wayne Go Away: Living in Fear of a Former Colleague," and "Never the Wayne Shall Meet: My Restraining Order Against Wayne Colt, Coke Fiend."

I immediately got a call from *The Daily Show*. I had made it to the Big Time, so I moved to the Big City and bought the Big House.

Now I had real responsibilities. If something goes wrong with your house, it's your problem. And boy, can things go haywire. There's electricity and fuse boxes and three-prong outlets. It's like living in the Space Station. No one warned me that life would involve science, except my science teacher. But, of course, he's going to say that. He's got a job to protect.

Four months after moving in, I noticed that the yard looked terrible. When we did the final walk-through, the lawn was beautiful. Now the grass was waist high and shaggy. Had I been sold a bill of goods? I faced the problem like a man and I called my lawyer.

He called a landscaper.

Now I knew a lot of yard guys were illegal immigrants—Blue-Collar Banditos stealing manual labor jobs away from Americans who had moved onto something less strenuous. So I let them do the lawn, then asked to see their green cards. They didn't have any, so I went inside and called INS. When Los Federales rolled up, I shouted from the window, "Enjoy mowing Mexico!"

It was an ugly scene. Turns out, they didn't have green cards because they were all Americans. In fact, African-Americans. I explained that I don't see Race. On that subject, I am very enlightened—and equally *endarkened*. Eventually, everything was smoothed over with some sizeable tips to the landscapers, and to the cops.

I tell this story to illustrate the issues we all face as American Adults. I call them the four Ss and one M of Maturity: Socioeconomics, Segregation, Science, Sombreros, and the Media.

fig 12. **STEPHEN COLBERT**

★ ★ ★

CHAPTER 10

THE MEDIA

"I read the news today. Oh boy."
–John Lennon, Liverpudlian flash-in-the-pan

 **FIRST JOB IN THE NEWS GAME WAS WRITING THE POLICE BLOTTER FOR THE DORCHESTER COUNTY PENNY-SAVER IN MY HOME STATE OF SOUTH CAROLINA. I WAS 17, AND I WAS HUNGRY. I'D HANG OUT AT THE LOCAL PRECINCT, PORING OVER POLICE REPORTS AND SWAPPING WAR STORIES WITH THE BOYS IN BLUE.**

Great bunch of guys—Seamus, Mickey, Potato Bill, Old Whiskey Pat, New Whiskey Pat, Paddy, and "Irish" (the black guy). It was a great way to hone my journalistic chops while learning about Law and Order. I took the job seriously, and I did it well. Recently, I unearthed my first column from its frame on my wall:

🛡 Police Blotter by Stephen "Tater" Colbert

LOITERING: At 1:44 am Tuesday, an Officer pursued two suspects believed to be playing loud music in the parking lot behind Durant Hardware at Vandberg Avenue. The suspects were described as two males in their late teens. (Sounds like Hispanics to me.)

NARCOTICS: A suspicious person was reported loitering outside a gas station near the bus depot. (Probably somebody waiting for drug dealers —maybe a couple of loud Hispanic drug dealers? Come on, America! Control the borders!)

ROBBERY: An elderly Rosinville resident, 79, told police that somebody might have entered her residence and moved items around. Nothing appeared to be missing. (Tip: She might want to check her ketchup. It may have turned into *salsa*. I'm just saying, if you want to keep ants out of the picnic basket, you build a fence.)

Feel free to cut this out and frame it on your wall.

No American editors
wanted that job?

My editor, Mr. Salinas, let me go after one column. This was my first cold, hard lesson in how "telling it like it is" isn't always "appreciated like it is." And I'd say not much has changed in the news game since then. I've faced the same prejudices against my in-your-face, take-no-prisoners style at every job along the way.[1]

The Bad News: The greatest threat facing America today—next to voter fraud, the Western Pinebark Beetle, and the memory foam mattress—is the national news media.

That doesn't mean
you're off the hook,
iodized salt.

Simple Question with a "Yes" answer: Is the mainstream press too liberal?

Hint: Yes

The answer is Yes.

Need proof? Just look at some of the headlines I'm able to imagine.

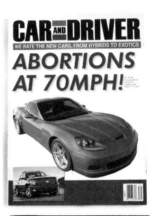

[1] Evidently, playing Kaiser Roll Basketball with the deep-fat frier is too "out there" for the Arby's Corporation.

The Good News: There are a few journalists who aren't registered sex offenders. These people work for Fox News. Now, I have a well-cured beef with Fox. "Fair *and* Balanced?" Which is it? Make up your mind! I'm sure guys like Brit Hume and Sean Hannity are well-intentioned, but by trying to present both sides of each story, they're suggesting that the truth exists somewhere in the middle. You know what's *really* in the middle?

A cream filling?

The Gray Area.

Shades of gray are for brain tissue and the weak. Neither one has a place in the News Business.

I like my Truth like my coffee: Black or White.

Wake Up Call: If I die, I know that I'm either going to Heaven or to Hell. *Heaven, just to be clear* There's no gray area there.

THE TOP MAINSTREAM MEDIA NEWS OUTFITS
THAT ARE KILLING OUR CHILDREN

NPR: What's wrong with NPR? Just listen to *Morning Edition*. This is by far the least zany "Morning Zoo" ever to hit the airwaves. Instead of the get-up-and-go-larity provided by your local Scott and Tom, or Ted and Zeke, or Denise and Santana, or Coyote Mike and The Beemer, *Morning Edition* presents NPR's measured barbiturate vibe.[2]

"Count your Chickens! Coyote's on the Prowl!" – Z 98.6 Body Temperature Rock!

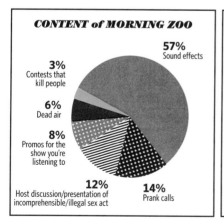

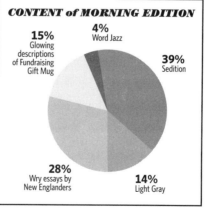

---

[2] *Fun Fact: NPR broadcasts at the same frequency as a coma patient's brainwaves.*

Lefties get up on the wrong side of the bed. The left side. It's a wonder the lefties who wake up to it are able to get out of bed.

I guarantee that if *Morning Edition* had to compete in the free market, you'd hear a lot more prank phone calls to the Supreme Court asking if that's a gavel "in their docket."

WHAT DOES NPR REALLY STAND FOR? Toss a few of these out at the next East Coast Ivy League Cocktail party you get roped into, and watch Billy Bleeding Heart choke on his brie.[3]

Nancy Pelosi Radio, Nader Presidential Radio, Nazi Palestinian Radio, No Penis Radio, Natalie Portman Radio

Try "Nasty Panda Radio" (It fits.)

N_____ P_____ Radio (Let your imagination soar!)

THE "BIG THREE" NETWORKS

Katie Couric

CBS: The Tiffany network is responsible for the perennial Sunday Night Post-Game buzzkill, *60 Minutes*. Morley Safer and his team of aged jackals present what I believe is the worst kind of investigative journalism—the kind with investigations. On the other hand, I like the innovations that Katie Couric has brought to *The CBS Evening News*, especially the innovation of having viewers turn elsewhere for news.

Brian Williams

NBC: A lot of people make the mistake of getting their nightly newscast from Brian Williams, when the real star of the "Peacock" news division is the *Law and Order* franchise. All the plots are "ripped from today's headlines."

Charlie   Charles

ABC: When Charlie Gibson took the evening news anchor chair, I doubted he had the heft for the job. But those fears were put at ease once I learned he had changed his name to "Charles Gibson." As far as liberal bias is concerned, jury's still out.

Jury's back in: Guilty!

Catch me on BookTV! Oct. 3rd! **CSPAN**: CSPAN's liberal bias is severely underestimated. With its unvarnished gavel-to-gavel coverage of our elected leaders, CSPAN glamorizes big government by showing not only how it works, but that it sometimes *does* work. CSPAN 2 may be just as dangerous, but has never been watched.

---

154   [3] *"Soft-cheese asphyxiation" is the 2nd leading cause of death among intellectuals, after "drinking with Christopher Hitchens."*

THE DORCHESTER COUNTY PENNYSAVER: Peaked for one week in 1981. (See page 151)

THE NEW YORK TIMES: One of the few downsides to my job is that I have to read *The New York Times* every day. Why? To quote my old friend Wesley "Irish" Snipes, "Know thine enemy." I do this dirty work as a service to my viewers, as the *Times'* cornucopia of bias and lies provide an endless source of things for me to be outraged about. And outrage is what makes me go. I call it "The Juice" because like steroids, *The New York Times* fills you with rage and shrinks your genitalia.

Or so I've heard

And—get this—there isn't even a comics page in *The New York Times*. I think that says all anyone needs to know about The Somber Gray Lady. Evidently, the Ochs and the Sulzburgers and the Dowds and the Krugmans think they're above it all. They look down on regular folk like you and me who delight at Garfield's lasagna-fueled "Cat-itude." So I'm forced to fashion my own Grin Bin by making up funny captions to photos in the International section. Here's one to tape to your cubicle!

LICENCE AND REGISTRATION, PLEASE

THE LIGHT AT THE END OF THE TUNNEL VISION

Over the last few years, the Internet has grown from a haven for pornography and pet anecdotes into a haven for pornography and pet anecdotes where people go for news. The source-checking, story-verifying, reality-worshiping dinosaurs of the mainstream media are being pushed aside by the emergent tree shrews of the blogosphere.

Evolution is a farce, but Evolution metaphors come in handy.

Do I have any hard data to back these claims up?

No, but I posted this on the Internet:

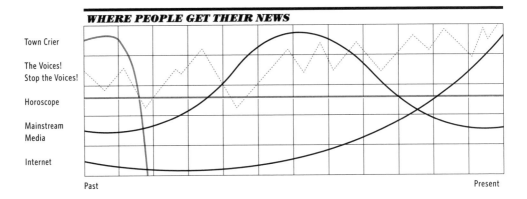

The beauty of new media is that no evidence is necessary. The brave blog-troopers have stormed the cockpit of news, and wrested the joystick of authority away from the seasoned pilots of the press who would land our country at Facts International Airport. Now there's fresh blood at the controls, without any of the preconceived notions of the rudder-and-flaps crowd.

With their Pro-Landing-Gear Agenda

This is the age of the open-source encyclopedia. Words like "research" and "corroborated" now mean whatever the majority says they mean. Personally, I'm voting for "research" to mean "speculation" and "corroborated" to mean "a zesty sour cream-based dip."

Example:

Recent *research* indicates that Barack Obama's ties to Al Qaeda have been *corroborated*. And they are delicious on baby carrots.

But if you ask me, and you implicitly did ask me by buying this book, the digital bloom may soon be off the virtual rose. These days even Wolf Blitzer covers blogs on his show, and the first thing every journalist learns is the five "W's" of journalism:

Who, What, When, Where, and

Wolf-Blitzer-is-for-hospital-patients-and-old-people.

STEPHEN SPEAKS FOR ME
A CHANCE FOR AVERAGE AMERICANS TO AGREE WITH WHAT I THINK

Amy Anatoly
Canton, Ohio

Hi! I'm Amy!

To be honest, I don't watch much TV news. The 24-hour cable stations focus too much on garbage I don't want my kids to see. And what with working as a cashier at ShopCo, I don't have time to read a newspaper. So, I mostly get my news from *Time* and *Newsweek* and *Modern Bride* and the other news weeklies on the rack. A glance at their covers is all I need to keep me in touch with what's going on in the world.

And let me tell you, it is a mess. Just look at Iraq. "Can We Win?" Or "Is It Too Late to Win the War?" I guess it all depends on "How Soon We Can Get Out." "Looking for a Way Out" is part of "The Way Out," but we can't forget there are "6 Ways to Fix It" and "75 Ways to Make Your Wedding Fabulous!" I think everybody over there just needs to "Stress Less, Relax More" and "Have Vacation Sex Without Leaving Home!"

Plus, from what I gather, "The Search for Historical Jesus" is going no better than "The Search for the Real Jesus" or even "The Search for Jesus." And until we find Jesus, "The Search for Mary" seems like jumping the gun.

Of course, we've got problems here at home, too. I have to wonder, "Toxic Toys? Are Kids Safe?" For that matter, "Are Kids Too Wired For Their Own Good?" "Do Kids Have Too Much Power?" "Are We Giving Kids Too Many Drugs?" But, most importantly, "Do We Care About Our Kids?"

One thing's for sure. We should all "Be Worried. Be Very Worried." Especially because, even though our brains are "Wired for Worry," no one really knows "Why We Worry About the Wrong Things." "Is Anything Safe?"

It gets so bad that some days, the only thing that gives me hope is that "Space Tourism May Be Closer Than You Think!"

Well, that's my break. Gotta get back to the Express Lane. Lotta pressure. See you "Inside the iPhone!"
Bye!

DEAR AMY,
THANKS SO MUCH FOR YOUR CONTRIBUTION!
NO FURTHER CONTACT PLEASE!
SINCERELY,
STEPHEN COLBERT

Gut Teaser™
THE "LIMO PROBLEM"

A limo driver has been dispatched to bring Tucker Carlson, James Carville and A Boston Cream Pie from MSNBC headquarters in New Jersey to a big-time press event in Manhattan.

Unfortunately, due to cutbacks at MSNBC, the limo can only carry one thing at a time. The limo driver can't leave Carlson alone with Carville, because Carville is insane and will attack and destroy Carlson, and of course one can't leave a Boston cream pie alone with Tucker Carlson. How will the pundits and the dessert get across the Hudson River to the event?

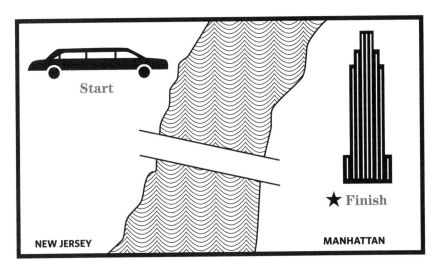

FUN  ZONE

OP-ED Illusion

Is this Bob Novak arguing with Paul Begala, or just a very poorly constructed vase?

Newsmedia Mix-em-up!

Descramble these names from the news media, then use the circled letters to solve the riddle.

TKCREU

☐◯◯☐◯☐☐

TINAHNY

☐◯☐◯◯◯◯

NOD MUSI

☐◯☐ ◯☐☐◯

POCORE

☐◯◯☐☐☐

"The ◯◯◯◯◯◯◯◯◯ ◯◯◯◯"

"Where Blitzer eats breakfast?"

fig 13. STEPHEN COLBERT

★ ★ ★

CHAPTER 11

CLASS WAR

"We're moving on up! To the East Side! To a De-luxe Apartment in the Sky!"
–George Jefferson, Dry Cleaner and Civil Rights Leader

FROM THE HEART: LET ME TELL YOU A STORY. GROWING UP, I LIVED IN A CLASSIC AMERICAN NEIGH-BORHOOD. IT WAS A MELTING POT OF HARDWORKING IRISH, BRITISH, ENGLISH, SCOTTISH, SCOTS-IRISH, WELSH AND NORTHERN IRISH. EACH MORNING, MY POP WOULD RISE AT THE CRACK OF DAWN

More of a "melting keg."

and walk a mile to pretend he was going to the store to pick up our breakfast. In the winter months, he'd chop down a neighbor's woodshed so we would have fuel to burn. When he got home, he would polish our shoes. If we couldn't afford shoes, he'd polish our feet. Then he'd send us off to school, with our sack lunches of pinecones and salt. Once he knew we were taken care of, he'd leave for his job working for the local rich guy.

*Don't ruin the text. Let your tears fall **here***

All day in class, I would think about what my dad did for us, how hard he worked, and that I never wanted to do any of that. I wanted to be the local rich guy. Today, I am.[1]

---

[1] *If you're late one more time, you're fired, Dad.*

REALITY CHECK: What is the point of my story? Through clean living, moral fortitude, and the foresight to narc out Channel 7's coke-addicted news anchor, and then take his job and win a regional Emmy for my coverage of his downward spiral, I changed my class status. That's right, folks. I'm talking about Class.

Also, Mike the prompter guy? Hopped up on Screamers

WHAT IS CLASS? Class is a way of looking at society that divides people into different categories based on how much money they're willing to make.

England has 2: Cockneys and Guv'ners.

> **BY THE NUMBERS:** Every society has its own class structure with a unique number of classes. France has five: Les Aristocrats, Les Bourgeoisie, Les Petit-Déjeuners, Les Grand Mal, and Les Moonves. India has one of the most rigid and complex class structures. Based upon their behavior in past lives, all Indians are born into different stratas of society called "castes." These castes forever determine what level of tech support questions they are allowed to answer.

Middle class: get off the fence. We're at War. Pick a side.[2]

We in America have three classes: Upper, Middle and Lower.

When I was growing up, we were in the Lower, and today, I'm in the Upper.

SO WHICH CLASS ARE YOU?

Ever have a nagging suspicion that you're poor? I know my staff does. And that's one of the reasons I devised this handy "Know Your Class" chart.

Class distinctions aren't just used to figure out where you sleep on a cruise ship. They are also used by pollsters and advertisers to better understand our buying habits.

If you know which class you belong to, you know which commercials you should pay attention to.

---

162 [2] *To future readers: I assume we're at war with someone.*

INSTRUCTIONS

For each question, circle the response that's closest to your answer. Good Luck.

QUESTION	LOWER	MIDDLE	UPPER
What keeps you up at night?	Sound of your own weeping	Growing suspicion you've been duped	"Should my topiary animals be alpha-betized by plant or by animal they represent?"
Retirement activities	Diabetes	Unable to retire thanks to children's educations	Alternating rounds of golf and plastic surgery
Your annual Federal tax bill	0	$25,000	0
Favorite drink	Grain alcohol and Robitussin	Chardonnay	Human Growth Hormone
Plan for accruing wealth	Powerball ticket	Scrimping and saving	Continuing to breathe
What did you eat for breakfast?	High fructose corn syrup	Whatever Jenny Craig said I could	Scrambled Fabergé Eggs
Where did you go on your last vacation?	The fire escape	Mall of America	Private island that's shaped like me
What sports do you play?	Gun Ball	Softball team spon-sored by bar you hide from family in	Training show dogs to play polo
What TV show best reflects your life?	Any broadcast with Anderson Cooper on the edge of tears	*Everybody Loves Raymond*	History Channel: *Finding Nazi Gold!*
What kind of shoes do you wear?	$175 Nike Air Force 25 Supremes	Whatever Payless had in my size	No shoes. Had the yard leathered.
TOTAL SCORE:			

Now count up your circled answers by column.

The column with the most circles is your class!

(If you feel like your answer is in between two responses, making you, say, "upper-middle class," you should remember that the phrase "upper-middle class" is a meaningless term created by the Upper class to keep the Middle class from joining with the Lower class when the Revolution comes.)

Based on your score, fill in the blanks.

"I, ... , am .... class."

(Name Here)

Introduce yourself this way from now on, and you'll quickly learn if you're at the right party.

WANT TO CHANGE YOUR CLASS? HERE'S HOW.

As a pundit, it's my job to fight for the little guy. In terms of the percentage of population, that means the Upper class. But all Americans are important to me. I won't be satisfied until everyone is in the top one percent.

Don't tell the poor about the escalator.

See, we're lucky here in America. We live in a free market society. Think of it as a ladder. No matter what rung you're born on, you have the exact same opportunity as everyone else to get to the top. Sure, you might say that some folks have less distance to climb than others, or that many of the lower rungs are slippery because they're covered with garbage and your high school didn't have an AP Ladder Climbing class, and the rung right above you is out of order and your landlord keeps saying he's going to fix it but he never does and all the while the guy who hangs out on the corner of your rung is constantly trying to get you high, and you're wondering if maybe you could get a little help up this ladder? Well, Mister, all the help you need is at your fingertips, if your fingertips are touching your ankles. I'm talking about bootstraps.

When life hands you a farm, make Farm-Aid.

You can always pull yourself up by your bootstraps or turn the lemons life has given you into lemonade.

Clearly, America has no shortage of metaphorical opportunities for the poor.

But some people would rather stay poor just to make us feel guilty. Well, don't look for any sympathy here. Instead of getting rich and paying their *No sympathy here either* own way, they'd rather go on welfare, and the liberals are more than happy to give it to them.

Now, I'm not the smartest knife in the spoon, so explain this to me. We're supposed to help folks out of poverty by *giving them a financial reward for being poor?* Doesn't add up. If being poor is a never-ending money party, where's the incentive to get rich?

Answer me this: what's going to help a shiftless vagabond more, a page of food stamps or the page from this book where I explain the free market "ladder"?

Hint: My paragraph gives him **motivation** and maybe even teaches him what a ladder is.

AT THIS POINT: You're probably wondering why I titled this chapter "Combat of the Class Commandos: The Coming Cashpocalypse." My editor may have changed it to something else. But he'll regret it. Publishing 101: Alliteration sells books. (I spent hours trying to make that rule alliterative, but it's impossible.)

Buy book. Big bargain, bro.

> **GUT SPEAKING:** Now some people might say it's callous not giving food stamps to poor people. They would say it's just another example of class warfare. Well, there *is* no class war in this country. The Upper class has such a tactical advantage that if the Lower class makes a sudden move we'll have a class massacre.

"Classacre" for short

If you ask me, the Upper class shows admirable restraint. They could easily freeze out the poor and man their factories with robots or mice. Instead, they offer them the opportunity for a decent wage, and up to two bathroom breaks. *If you're reading this in the bathroom, get back to work!*

But do folks in the Lower classes respond with even a simple gesture of gratitude like giving up a decent wage and one of those bathroom breaks? No. Instead, they form unions, which they use to bully our nation's factory owners with walkouts, strikes, and that one Sally Field movie where she plays a labor organizer with sixteen personalities. *Steel Magnolias?*

ARE YOU IN A UNION? *(Please circle one)*   Yes   No

Thank you for filling out my labor questionnaire. If you circled "yes," know that I could have you replaced with a single phone call. There are hundreds of scabs out there who can read my book just as well as you can. Don't tempt me.

Don't feel guilty, scabs. You help with the healing.

WILL YOU TEMPT ME? *(Please circle one)*   Yes   No

I trust you made the right choice.

CANARY IN A COAL MINE

Take a look at this little tit bit I found in *The Chicago Tribune:*

Seems some enviro-"mental" group, the Ecology Center, is claiming that the new-car smell we all crave is actually a deadly cocktail of chemical pollutants:

That New-car Smell May Be Newest Hazard

Of primary concern are bromine used for flame retardants, chlorine used in plasticizers and lead used in plastics, as well as arsenic, copper, mercury and nickel that have been linked to allergies, birth defects, impaired learning, liver toxicity and cancer.

Now at first I thought this was just another buzz-shackle attempt by the envious hippie nut-jobs who can't afford a new car every season because chaining yourself to a maple tree doesn't pay what it used to in the 60s.

But then it hit me: something more insidious was going on here. Who spends a lot of time breathing in that new-car smell? **The Upper Class.**

Who's loading those cars up with toxic chemicals? Factory Workers. **The Lower Class.**

So are we in a Class War? I don't know, but if we are, it's pretty clear who just fired the first shot.

A SURPRISING ADMISSION

Sometimes I envy the folks in the Lower classes. Like the kid I was pretending to be in the story I made up at beginning of this chapter. They have so much to look forward to. Their bootstraps are so loose and fit for pulling. Mine can't go any tighter. I'm losing circulation as it is.

But poor people have a very precious gift: something to strive for. But I've got nothing left to reach for because I've been so successful at everything I've put my hands on. Sometimes I can't think of a reason to get out of bed in the morning. *The Midas grope* Luckily for me, I have a motorized bed. I like to drive it down to the rough side of town and give the people on the streets inspiration to work harder.

STEPHEN SPEAKS FOR ME
A CHANCE FOR AVERAGE AMERICANS TO AGREE WITH WHAT I THINK

**Thomas Bindlestaff,
Executive Assistant
to Mr. Stephen Colbert**

I am living Proof that the American Dream is Possible! UPward mobility exists in this land of oPPortunity!

ExPlanatory note: I aPologize, but my tyPewriter keyboard is missing the lowercase letter "P." As my job is to make tyPewritten coPies of all of Mr. Colbert's Personal corres Pondence, you might think this would Prove challenging. Fortunately, Mr. Colbert rarely uses lowercase letter "P's," and when he does, I simPly remove the sheet of PaPer from the tyPewriter, reinsert the sheet of PaPer uPside-down, tyPe a lowercase "d," remove it again, reinsert it rightside uP and then Proceed as I had been Proceeding Previously, desPite my Painful and Persistent Penman's Gout.

As I was saying, I'm movin' uP! Already I make nearly $18,000 a year! And sooner or later (sooner, I dearly hoPe), I shall be the family's first self-made twenty-thousan-daire! In "Colbert Bucks," that is.

Like all Mr. Colbert's emPloyees, my salary is Paid in company ScriP. Mr. Colbert has thoughtfully Provided a comPany store with a variety of fine dry goods. It has all the essentials: flour, salt, corn meal, rendered beef tallow, ticking and burlaP. My wife has her eye on a tin of baking Powder. The ladies do love to dream!

Oh! There's the whistle! Is it dawn already? I must get started on Mr. Colbert's corresPondence. His rePresentative may be in today. I need to make a good imPression. I'm hoPing to get my youngest a Position with the firm removing debris from the hydraulic ram shaft.

Only the wee ones will fit. Note to self: cut back on his ration of suet. Mark my words! I swear by the curvature of my sPine, someday I shall be rich!

Your Humble Servant,
Thomas Bindlestaff

FUN ZONE

How many differences can you find in these pictures?

★ ★ ★

CHAPTER 12

RACE

"Ebony and Ivory, live together in perfect harmony,
Side by side on my piano keyboard."

–Paul McCartney and Stevie Wonder, the surviving Beatles

IS SOMETHING INTERESTING ABOUT WHAT MISTERS WONDER AND MCCARTNEY STUMBLED UPON HERE IN THEIR JAUNTY TRIBUTE TO THE PIANO. WITH A LITTLE IMAGINATION, THE LYRICS CAN ALSO ACT AS A METAPHOR FOR RACE. THE WHITE KEYS COULD REPRESENT WHITE PEOPLE, AND THE BLACK keys could represent non-white people. Because in America, people of all colors live in perfect harmony.

Asians represented by "Chopsticks"

But it hasn't always been that way.

Once upon a time, racism was a terrible problem in this country,[1] and it's still a subject you're supposed to handle delicately.[2] Sorry, folks, that's not my style. I'm not afraid to disturb the skeletons in America's closet, no matter what race those skeletons are. (You can tell by measuring the eye-teeth.)

I'm not actually sorry.

I'm going to talk about race, and I'm not taking any racial prisoners.

NOT slaves

WHERE DID RACISM COME FROM?

Well, before the Civil War, skin color didn't matter, because all black people were slaves. But then after they were freed that name "slave" didn't really fit anymore, so former slaves started calling themselves "Black" or "Negro" or

---

[1] *Approximately from 1864 to the recording of "Ebony and Ivory."*
[2] *If race were a sweater, it would be made of cashmere, and you could only wash it by hand.*

"colored."[3] In short, skin began to matter, and, folks, racism was off to the races.

Suddenly, the world was divided. White people had their drinking fountains, and Black people had their drinking fountains. White people had their schools, and Black people had their drinking fountains.[4]

After about a hundred years of this, a very smart man named Dr. The Reverend Martin Luther King Jr. gave a speech and said, "I have a dream that this should end!"

And it did.[5]

May vary on a block-by-block basis

Racism no longer exists in America.

Don't believe me? Down in Selma, Alabama, they recently opened up The National Civil Rights Museum. It's all about the fight against racism. Well, folks, it stands to reason that you don't open a museum for something that still exists. Case in point: the Air and Space museum. Once we "landed on the moon," Air and Space was over. Scotchguard Neil Armstrong and hang him from the ceiling.

Museum gift shop sells "I have a dream" sleep mask.

But even though racism is over, for many people, sadly, race still exists. As long as any part of that word still lingers, we're all in trouble. So, how do we erase Race?[6] Let me tell you how I did it.

NEWS FLASH: I don't see race.[7]
THIS JUST IN: I used to see race.

Caught your breath yet? I'll say it again.

I. Used. To. See. Race. In fact, I used to see it everywhere. I was very good at it, if I'm to believe what people shouted at me.

My struggle

But all that changed the day I read Ralph Ellison's thought-provoking novel *Invisible Man*. I found myself deeply moved by his tale of a black scientist who, through no fault of his own, becomes invisible and is driven mad.

---

172 [3] *I'm pretty sure there are other terms, but my publicist insists that there aren't.*
[4] *The stereotype ends **now**. Black people DO NOT drink more water than other races.*
[5] *With the help of Stevie Wonder and Paul McCartney.*
[6] *eRace is a registered trademark of Stephen Colbert's web-based diversity program.*
[7] *In the same way I assume that everybody is White, I assume that every traffic light is green. This sort of positive thinking gets me home 15 minutes sooner.*

Reading *Invisible Man* made me realize something very important: If you're invisible, it means you're the same color as air. And air has no color. Then it hit me: If race is no longer to divide us, our races all need to be invisible!

So, maybe until that great day when all humans can't see color,[8] those with darker skin should take the Invisible Man's brave example and wrap themselves in the white bandages of unity so that we all truly look the same color. *Albinos, you're halfway there.*

You see, White people are already wrapped in bandages: the skin God gave us to protect us from racism. People of all colors deserve no less.

MY VISION OF A RACE-FREE FUTURE

Burn victim or Black guy?
(It shouldn't matter!)

> **REMEMBER:** While skin and race are often synonymous, *skin* cleansing is good, *race* cleansing is bad.

---

[8] *I don't see color, but I do see luster, and people with a semi-gloss finish are lazy.*

We're all the same. Unfortunately, not everyone sees that. They get too hung up on little things like "appearance" and "history" and "cultural identity." In fact…

I prefer to divide people by brand-loyalty.

Some People seem to think racism still exists. These people are racists. What's their angle? I say follow the money. They have something to gain from keeping the race game afloat. What is it?

BLIGHTS! SCAM-ERA! AFFIRMATIVE ACTION!

Affirmative action is a prime example of the Leftist campaign to make ideas seem less dangerous than they are, through the strategic use of positive words.

Like " living wage"

Think about it. How can something be bad if it is "affirmative"? And how can we ignore it if it is "action"?[9] See, its name does nothing to describe what "affirmative action" actually is: a system that rewards Group A and punishes Group B just because long ago something bad happened to Group A that incidentally made Group B a whole lot of money.

One of my mottos is, "Never make a decision because you feel guilty." The bleeding hearts that came up with affirmative action back in the anything-goes 1960s could have used my advice. They felt bad about the racial injustices of the past, so they decided to make it a crazy law that gave minorities preferential treatment when it came to the choicest jobs, scholarships, and roster spots on NBA teams.

Short version: "Never feel guilty."

Stay strong, NHL!

> **GUT SPEAKING:** The worst thing about affirmative action is that it encourages **reverse discrimination**, so-called because it goes in the opposite way of how we naturally discriminate.

Like friendship, discrimination is a two-way street.

Here's a typical story: A well-qualified young White man doesn't get into the College of His Choice, but has a strong suspicion that a lot of Black guys might have. It gets worse: A hard-working White employee is passed over for a promotion in favor of a coworker who seems like he could be gay. What's next? Should there be affirmative action in my bedroom? Should Chinese guys get a shot at my wife just because the conditions on the Transcontinental Railroad weren't *ideal*?

But the worst thing about affirmative action is that it's Big Government intruding into the world of business. I don't need some bureaucrat telling me to be an equal opportunity employer. When it comes to job applicants at the *Report*, race is irrelevant. All they have to do is answer a skill-testing questionnaire:

Sample Question:

Question 43: We're shooting an episode of *The Colbert Report* at the beach. It's a very sunny day. What number SPF sunblock do you use? Support your answer:

_____

_____

When it comes to affirmative action, I quote myself: "Hogwash!" However, most people quote noted beagle-abuser President Lyndon Johnson, who summed up his stance on the issue with the following analogy: "Imagine a hundred yard dash in which one of the two runners had his legs shackled together. He has progressed ten yards, while the unshackled runner has gone fifty yards. How do they rectify the situation? Do they merely remove the shackles and allow the race to proceed?…Would it not be the better part of justice to allow the previously shackled runner to make up the forty-yard gap, or to start the race all over again?"[10]

The press was a lot easier to entertain in 1964.

---

[10]   *He actually said this.*

Johnson was right on one point: Racial issues in this country deserve the same amount of attention we give track and field events.

While Johnson's idea was terrible for public policy, he stumbled upon what I think would be a great improvement for track and field: shackles! How exciting would it be to give each runner a unique, massive obstacle to overcome!

Here's how I see the 100 yard dash of tomorrow:

LANE

1. A shackled runner
2. Runner forced to wear a sandwich board
3. Runner in ice skates
4. Runner must run backward holding a hand mirror
5. Runner's pockets filled with sausages with a pack of wild, angry dogs released on the field
6. Bare feet on a lane of wet bathroom tile— responsible for 80% of household fatalities!
7. Runner given horrible news moments before start— I mean really bad
8. Death row inmate running on his knees. If he wins, he's freed!

"Your grandmother is on fire."

Just a reminder: None of these are metaphors. I want to see this actually happen.

> **PROOF I'M NOT A RACIST:** George Washington Carver had some pretty good ideas, like corrective lenses for peanuts.

If you suffer from peanut allergies, turn the page quickly.

 # STEPHEN SPEAKS FOR ME

A CHANCE FOR AVERAGE AMERICANS TO AGREE WITH WHAT I THINK

**Rev. George A. Lewis,
Ex-Civil Rights Leader**

Shout it from the loftiest mountaintops and through the deepest valleys: Racism is no more! Bigotry, that grim hydra, which once reared its heads in every corner of our proud society, infecting all Americans with its venomous bite, has been vanquished. And I have done my part to slay it.

I marched on Washington shoulder-to-shoulder with Dr. King. I labored alongside Reverend Jackson in Chicago. I was instrumental in bringing integration to the University of Alabama, and thanks in part to my actions, racism gave way to equality, oppression to justice, and segregation to brotherhood.

But as justice rose like a mighty tide from the Mississippi delta to the highest corridors of power, my own sense of purpose receded. What is a Civil Rights leader to do once Civil Rights have been permanently achieved?

For a while, I returned to full-time Reverending. But being a preacher is hard work, and let's face it, without racism to rail against, my sermons didn't have the same zazz.

So I left my church and sought new causes to champion.

I tried marching alongside another oppressed group, the homosexuals. But then I found out what they did when they weren't marching.

Other protests proved no better fit. I couldn't in good conscience join the No-Nukes movement, because I'm a firm believer in America's nuclear first strike capabilities. And I'd rather not recount the lack of appetite for political change at the St. Patrick's Day Parade.

After that, I flailed around a bit. I remained committed to the principles of non-violence, but I adapted it to the injustices I encountered in the new post-racist world. I organized a sit-in to protest the unfair practices of a local restaurant. ($13.00 for a spicy tuna roll? Come on!) But it failed to achieve change.

I grew isolated and disconsolate. And as painful as it is to admit, in the depths of my despair I once tried to reintroduce racism, but those Korean grocers would not rise to my bait.

As of this writing, I am unemployed, and let me tell you, the pension benefits offered by the Civil Rights Movement are meager at best. I am currently available to fight for the downtrodden, freelance mass-rallying, and light roof repair.

In the immortal words of Dr. King, "Free at last! Free at last! Thank God Almighty, I'm free at last." If only he had known the cost.

FUN  ZONE

SLUR FIND

```
D F U I K N M N N O P L K S K M O
S D K I N H C G H N M K C E D O J
E C N B J I K O M O T S E L C N U
D X U W N K P A M A W X N E W W E
A R H N I J Z X S P I C D X K R A
P A O E I L O O C C N E E C Z E E
S G B Q S B N N C D K X R U B D L
W H P J W U O H J I I W H R K S L
C E M K O O L D R W E T B A C K M
R B H A O L P X M N W S Y E M I L
E V M I C K W E S M H E K I K L W
N C P E K X M S I O Y F N I L P W
A M S I D A R K Y W M T O W E L H
L O D G K R O V B Y P O Y H M E R
L P I L D F M X P O L A C K K M G
V N J M K I E A A G C N I O L R M
J P I N H I M X S L C J M W P D O
```

How many racial slurs can you find in the grid above?

Answer: Zero. Why? Do you see some, racist?

CHAPTER POSTSCRIPT

When I say I don't see race, I mean I don't see Black people.

But I can spot a Mexican a hundred paces.

Read on!

★ ★ ★

CHAPTER 13

IMMIGRANTS

"You don't have to live like a refugee."

–Tom Petty, who doesn't because he's an <u>American</u>

WE ARE BEING COLONIZED BY AN INVADING FORCE! DID YOU KNOW THAT THERE ARE MORE ILLEGAL MEXICAN IMMIGRANTS IN AMERICA TODAY THAN THERE WERE AMERICAN TROOPS IN OCCUPIED GERMANY AFTER WORLD WAR II? UNLIKE MOST OF MY FACTS, I CAN BACK THAT ONE UP WITH REALITY.

Experts say there are 12 to 14 million illegal immigrants in the United States. To put that into perspective, if you took all the foreigners who have no business living in America and put them into Dodge Caravans (remember, those seat six) and drove them out of the country taking up all three lanes of a highway, the line of minivans would stretch for I don't *care* how long, because the more important question is: How can we get them into those vans?

GOOD NEWS: You won't need any documentation to get into my opinions on immigration, because through the very act of buying this book your identity has been electronically entered into a secret government registry.

We still need a urine sample, however.

DO WE HAVE A PROBLEM WITH ILLEGALS?

I'll say!

We have a problem with illegals.

Now a lot of people, including my spellcheck, have a problem with the term "illegals." They say it's not a word, and even if it were it would be insensitive to the feelings of the people who are breaking our nation's laws. Fine. Let's call them "immorals" because what could be more immoral than a Guatemalan crossing into this country to pick our American fruit just because her kids are poor?

I can hear the cries now: "How can you suggest that we slam the door?! America is a nation of immigrants!! We all have ancestors who left their crowded, impoverished homelands behind for America!!!! Even Andrew Carnegie was an immigrant!!!!!!!"

!!!!!!!!!!!!!!!!!!!!!!!!!!
!!!!!!!!

First of all, cool it with the exclamation marks.[1] The cost of this ink comes out of my advance. Second, it's interesting you should bring up Andrew Carnegie—one of our nation's most esteemed robber barons. Yes, he was born in Scotland. So what makes him different from the type of "immorals" we're experiencing today?

Uncover your ears and listen.

Once upon a Time, there was the *right* kind of foreigner.

Yes, Virginia, there is a right kind of foreigner. The kind who comes to America, loses his brogue and creates U.S. Steel. When he dies, he leaves the legacy of breaking the Homestead Strike of 1892, paving the road for non-union workers everywhere! If he admits to any foreign ties, it's to having a hunting estate at Skilbo Castle in Scotland. And that's it. No parades. No crazy hat dances. His only clubs are ones like "The South Fork Fishing and Hunting Club" whose manmade, trout-stuffed lake burst through its dam leaving 2,200 dead in one of the greatest floods in American history, the Johnstown Flood of 1889. Sad event, great social club. Over 60 millionaires, and that was back when trolley rides cost a penny.

I wonder what they cost today.

> **GUT SPEAKING:** Of course, we can't all be Andrew Carnegies, but we can honor the struggles and ambitions of our immigrant ancestors by doing as they did: leaving the past behind for the sake of a brighter future.

---

182 [1] *And don't you **dare** put any of them upside-down and in front of sentences.*

MY STRUGGLE: I am a member of a mixed-race marriage. While I am the proud product of hardy Irish Catholic stock, my wife is Scots Presbyterian. In the Old Country, our love could never have been. In fact, a glance at my wife's family records shows that her ancestors moved onto the very land my family was forced to abandon when that Roundhead son-of-a-bitch Oliver Cromwell forced the Irish west of the river Shannon to farm rocks. But when the Colbert clan set sail for America, they harbored two shining hopes: that they could survive a three-month steerage passage on coal-and-onion-peel soup; and that one day their children could forget the enmity of the past and live a life of freedom. I've done them one better. Seven generations on, I've "planted my Irish flag" on the very family that stole our land.

More like Crom-bad

See, the great thing about my marriage is that it symbolizes the hope America once offered its immigrants. Here, immigrants received a gift never given before in world history: They could leave the past behind. (Another less exciting gift was cholera.) How lucky they were to get to erase all remnants of their previous lives, languages and cultures and go about the business of becoming an American Christian.

Arrivederci, "Arrivederci"

So let's take that beautiful idea to its logical conclusion and not only leave the past behind but deny the past ever happened.[2] Like this:

America is <u>not</u> a land of immigrants.

There. Was that so hard to say? It makes sense if you think about it. It *feels* like we've been here forever, doesn't it? Let's just assume we have been.

How does it taste to smash the shackles of our past? It tastes like *freedom*.

And freedom doesn't need chipotle sauce

Now that we've liberated ourselves from the old factual myth of our immigrant history, we can focus on the future. And let me tell you, there are dark times ahead, because for the first time in our new history we are being swarmed by legions of *immigrants*.

---

[2] *What Alamo?*

And folks, it's time to fight back.

Also know government faked "Moon landing"

We all know the government has refused to take action to end the problem. It's up to us.

Here are three things we can do to secure the borders *today*.

1 **Heavily arm our volunteer militias.** The failure of leadership in Washington has given rise to a new border patrol of selfless patriots called the Minutemen. I have hung out with these guys. Let me assure you they take their duties deadly seriously. Let me also assure you that night-vision goggles are cool. Get a pair.[3]

The ponchos are coming! The ponchos are coming!

2 **Take a lesson from the Chinese.** We need to build a 2000-mile long wall along our southern border. This will have two benefits. First of all, when I'm worried I like to stay busy. Building a giant wall is a great way to keep the nation's mind off how many immigrants enter the country through airports. Second, this wall might actually keep people out. If it's built **right**, not like that picket fence the Russians threw up across Berlin. We don't want these Mexican Jumping Beans hopping over whenever they feel like it. Make it **tall**. I mean tall enough that if you bake at the top of it, you'd need to use the high-altitude instructions.[4] I'm talking about something that can be seen from space, with double-wall construction, machine-gun nests and a flaming moat loaded with fireproof crocodiles.

A lesson for us all

3 **You want to end the swarm, take away the honey pot.** Everybody says immigrants just do the jobs Americans don't want to do, but let's test that theory. They pick our fruits and vegetables. Who wouldn't want to have a job that got them out in the fresh air more often? Hell, I pay twenty bucks a pop for the privilege of picking apples and pumpkins every October. And the hay ride is extra!

[3] *SkyMall® has some great deals.*
[4] *And you'd better be baking an apple pie.*

If we really want to get rid of these occupational interlopers, I say we give them the jobs *nobody* wants to do. Here are a few American jobs that will have them packing their piñatas in no time:

- **Pottery Teacher:** Feel like throwing yourself in front of a train? Throw a pot instead! The one word that will best describe your students is "desperate-middle-aged-woman-looking-for-a-creative-outlet-after-the-divorce." A word that won't describe them, however, is "talented." There are only so many ways of patiently asking "What are you trying to make?" before you finally snap and use the kiln to cook a car battery.

This was supposed to be a plate.

- **High School Guidance Counselor:**[5] You wake up every morning thinking "If I'm so good at finding careers, how did I end up with this one?" At least you're not the Vice Principal.

- **Bass Player:** It's like you made a poorly worded deal with the devil to be a rock star. Instead of fame, fortune and groupies, you stand in the shadows plucking one note for 90 minutes while the lead singer picks out a trio of coeds from the front row for a post-show pansexual trapeze act. Even worse, you're expected to room with the drummer.

Your groupies: Pottery students.

USEFUL WORD: Xenophobia, n., a fear of foreigners. <u>Not</u> a fear of Warrior Princesses. (Note: Not crazy about Warrior Princesses either. I like my damsels helpless and in a tower. Thanks, but I'll do the fighting, gals.)

I'M NOT A MONSTER: Let's face it—people in other countries lead horrible, pointless lives filled with hardship and strange brand names for their snack crackers.

---

[5] *My guidance counselor told me to follow my dreams, but it's hard to get a job as a dragonfly.*

CANARY IN A COAL MINE

You will never hear me criticize the Statue of Liberty. You can't get more American than her—that's why the French gave her up.

I can, however, criticize poetry. Just look at this item I saw in the *New York Sun*.

Misprint Is Spied In Lazarus Poem At Liberty Island
BY GARY SHAPIRO— Staff Reporter of the Sun

December 8, 2006

The Old Colossus

There appears to be an error on the bronze plaque inside the pedestal of the Statue of Liberty, inscribed with the famous sonnet "The New Colossus" by Emma Lazarus.
Lazarus's poem contains the immortal lines: "'Give me your tired, your poor, / Your huddled masses yearning to breathe free, / The wretched refuse of your teeming shore.'" Just prior to these lines on the plaque are inscribed the following lines: "'Keep ancient lands, your storied pomp!' cries she / With silent lips." But in the hand-written manuscript for a collection of poems that Lazarus compiled in 1886, a year before her death, the phrase "ancient lands" is set off by commas: " 'Keep, ancient lands, your storied pomp!' "

Whatever happened to the old adage, "Copy edit twice, cast in bronze once"? Now we've spent 120 years thinking our "pomp" should be keeping "ancient lands," instead of "ancient lands" keeping our "pomp"! That changes *everything*.

Up till now, this poem has always been interpreted to mean that we should throw our arms wide open to every Dutch Boy who wants to paddle his bong across the Atlantic.

But with the discovery of this error, who knows what in the hell Lazarus meant to say? Maybe there are other manuscripts of the poem out there with all different punctuation. Different words, even. There's no certainty anymore whether this statue was intended to be welcoming to immigrants at all. Maybe that torch isn't meant to be a beacon, but a searchlight to make it easier for the INS to spot people sneaking over the border.

I say, let's use this opportunity to replace the error-filled, unverifiable and troublesome Lazarus poem with something a little more in tune with the times. Something that's impossible to punctuate incorrectly.

STEPHEN SPEAKS FOR ME
A CHANCE FOR AVERAGE AMERICANS TO AGREE WITH WHAT I THINK

The Guy Sitting Next to You At The Stadium

Woooo! Hey, remember me from the Sports Chapter? Chevron —The Gas with Techron! Shut up Deb, I know this guy.

Anyway, I heard there was a job opening in this chapter, and frankly, I could use the work, what with all the Speedo Gonzaleses out in front of the Home Depot snatching up my construction jobs.

Let me tell you what illegal immigration has done to us guys in drywall—Hold up. They're doing the National Anthem. Deb, what are you doin'? You gotta stand up. Because it's the fucking National Anthem, that's why. Show some respect. Jesus fuck, Deb.

O the ramparts we watched, were so gallingly streaming! And the rocket's red glaaaare! Wooooooooooooo!

The bomb bursting out there, came truth with the night that our hmm-hmm who cares?!

Put your hand over your heart, Deb. Your *heart*. It's the thumpy thing under that left rosin bag of yours.

O THE LAND OF THE FREEEEE!!! It's go time! *AND THE HOOOOME... OF THE... BRAAAAAAAAAAAAAAAVE!*

PLAY GODDAMN BALL! Let's fucking DO this! WoooooOHOOOOOOOOOO!

You can sit down, Deb.

Those guys down on the field, they gotta go out and earn it every day. Your average drops below .200, they kick your ass right down to the minors. Same with America. If we let our average go down too low, I mean our average of real Americans, we'll end up like some minor league country, like Mexico or Guatelahala. That's what chuffs me about foreigners. They're bringin' our stats down.

Yo! Beer guy! Hey! Two beers here! Two *apiece*! Alright. Pass 'em this way. Keep 'em moving, keep 'em moving. Hey dipshit! Want to get your thumb out of my brew? Deb, drink yours quick. We'll do these now and then I'll go pick up some more between innings. Chug-a-fuckin'-lug.

Here's the exception. See who we got pitching today? Gutierrez. Hell of an arm. He can throw a ball of fucking *fire*. He's doing something *positive* for society. Hell, we should bring over his whole family on a raft and stick 'em right into Spring Training.

WHAT!? Come ooooonnnnnn—I could see that was a strike from up here! Eat some carrots, ump! You weak-eyed pussy fag fuck! BOOOOOOOOOOOOOOO! Come on, Deb. BOOOOOOOOOOO! That's it, baby.

Shit, yeah! That was a *sweet* grab. Right out of the vines. You know, couple years ago, I had my doubts about some of these Asian guys they brought over from the Orient. But that Matsumoto bastard is like a ninja in center field. He'd make a solid citizen.

Popped him UP! Popped-him-the-fuck up! Nice inning. That's what I like to see. Bing-boop de-doop. Threeup, threedown. Way to go, Gutierrez! Give that man a green card!

Be back with nachos.

They were out of nachos, so I got four more beers. Hey Deb, what did I miss? Well you'd know if you weren't yakkin' on that phone all the time. Was it Trish? I just *guessed*. You talk to her every fucking second, Deb. I'm not thinkin' about her, I just *guessed*. Jeez...

Come on, Gutierrez! Just like last inning—three up, three down! You the man! You the...Oh shit. Go foul...No...GO FOUL! Go the FUCK foul! God *Dammit!* Hey, GUTIERREZ! Go back to Mexico, YOU PUSSY-ARMED CHILI-SHITTIN' FUCK!

Who they puttin' in? Sanchez? Alright! A <u>Dominican</u>. Those guys can *play*. Let's fucking do this, amigo! Wooooooooooooooooooooo!

What does America need to help protect her porous borders from illegal immigrants?

Connect the dots to find the answer.

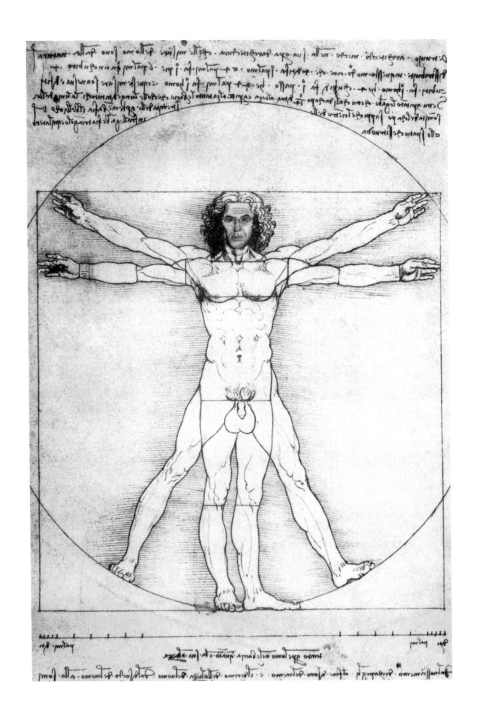

fig 16. STEPHEN COLBERT

★ ★ ★

CHAPTER 14

SCIENCE

"She blinded me with science."

–Thomas Dolby, unable to find scientific formula for follow-up hit

I MAY QUOTE MYSELF: REALITY HAS A WELL-KNOWN LIBERAL BIAS. AND WHO CAN YOU DEPEND ON TO KOWTOW TO REALITY LIKE IT'S THE ONLY GAME IN TOWN? SCIENTISTS. THEY DO IT RELIGIOUSLY. WITH THEIR FANATICAL DEVOTION, SCIENTISTS ARE NO BETTER THAN CULT MEMBERS—

Like Eve, Newton offended God with an apple.

only difference is that they put their blind faith in empirical observation instead of in a drifter who marries 14-year-olds and declares himself the reincarnation of Ramses II.

Now, I have nothing against observation per se. Looking at things is one of my great talents. In fact, as vice president of my Neighborhood Crime Watch, I personally witnessed a young couple attempt to paint their house a color not approved by the Home Owners' Association. Thanks to my observation and flier campaign, their gracious home is now a beautiful Mannered Taupe.

But scientists use observation in a different way: to draw conclusions about the way reality works. They look at the world and ask questions about it. Only problem, we weren't put on this planet to question our environment, we were put here to process it into fuel for our cars.

"Why am I so lonely?"

Kill two birds: add fabric softener and rat poison.

You see, like a load of dirty laundry spontaneously generates rats, questions spontaneously generate *data* and *facts*. And trust me: I wouldn't italicize these things if I didn't believe they were dangerous. It's not like I'm looking for extra work.

Just take a look at history. Over the centuries, scientific evidence has viciously attacked the status quo. There's a reason we have a status quo: It ensures that the *status* of our lives is consistent so we can meet our *quo*tas. When 18th-century scientist Edward Jenner discovered that parents could protect their children from smallpox with a vaccine, it may have saved a few thousand lives, but it also destroyed the magic amulet industry.

Science attacks our most cherished opinions. Opinions which come straight from our collective gut. Oh, wait, according to gastroenterologists, the only thing that comes from the gut is waste left from the digestion of food. That's right, "waste." I guess that means that scientists literally think our opinions should be flushed down the toilet!

Well, I'm not flushing and neither should you! In the last few centuries science has made some giant strides in our understanding of the world, but it's time to turn back the clock. Speaking of clocks, how about we stop letting the earth's rotation dictate what time it is? I say it's Morning in America![2]

"METHOD?" OR MADNESS?[3]

Bunsen burnouts

When it comes to understanding the universe, the Beaker Brigade won't shut up about its method of inquiry, **The Scientific Method.**[4]

Café Americano

This process consists of several basic steps, including but not limited to—I'm sorry, I blacked out there. Suffice it to say, there are a bunch of steps. Put on a pot of coffee. This might take a while.

> *Step 1: Observation:* "Mankind has a pretty nice relationship with God."

> *Step 2: Hypothesis:* "I bet people would start to doubt the existence of God if I claimed that the Earth revolves around the Sun, instead of the other way around like the Bible says."

---

192   [2] *It doesn't **feel** like we're rotating.*
[3] *Answer: Madness.*
[4] *Only good method: rhythm.*

Step 3: Experiment: "I will publish my heretical beliefs and see how the
Church reacts."

Step 4: Conclusion: "I recant! Please stop torturing me!!!"

Sorry—"Enhanced Interrogating" me

A BETTER WAY

It's natural to be curious about our world, but the scientific method is just one
theory about how to best understand it. We live in a democracy, which means
that we should treat every theory equally.

Just don't be curious about your body.

So here's an alternative two-step method for understanding the universe:

Step 1: **Remember:** Six thousand years ago, God created the
Heavens and the Earth.

Step 2: **Repeat as necessary.**

Step 3? Repent as necessary.

Isn't that a whole lot easier than analyzing electromagnetic background for
evidence of some "Big Bang" fourteen billion years ago? Fourteen billion is a
pretty big number, and God didn't create us so we could waste time trying to
picture fourteen billion cupcakes. *(DON'T TRY THIS!)*

One... two... aaargh!

MOVING ON: That about covers science, but what about the folks who
practice this crackpot doctrine? I spend a lot of time with scientists (about 6
minutes with each one that comes on my show), and I can honestly say that
despite appearances, most of them are decent, well-intentioned people. They're
just dangerously deluded. It's easy to see how they get sucked in. They're
physically awkward and lonely, so they spent their adolescence down by the
creek studying the creatures that live there. "I may be ridiculed at school," they
think, "but a *crayfish* would never judge me."[5]

However, Neil DeGrasse Tyson is an absolute monster.

So my heart goes out to them. Figuratively. I would never actually entrust
my heart to scientists—they'd probably implant it in a baboon. And a baboon
with my heart would be practically unstoppable. Baboon strength and agility
combined with <u>my</u> determination and media savvy? It would be a threat to all
of humanity.[6]

But a baboon with my hair would make a handsome pet.

---

[5] *Wrong! If that crayfish had bigger claws, it would pants you in a second.*
[6] *Not to mention baboonity.*

> **ELITE E-LERT:** Scientists claim that the earth is four billion years old. Yet they still can't explain many of the enduring mysteries of the universe. Hey, scientists, if you're so smart, why do you need more than four billion years to figure stuff out?

NO HEROES ALLOWED: I've said it before (see above), science is elitist. Making rules, setting boundaries, constantly telling us what is and isn't flammable[7]—all without input from the very people who are expected to abide by those laws. I know I never consented to Gravity Without Representation.

So who gave some lab-coated pipette wielder permission to act like he knows more than I do about mitochondria, just because he spent twenty years of his life studying them in a laboratory? PhDs and 300-page dissertations don't make his opinion any more valid. I happen to have some mitochondria myself, and I can tell you that *mine* don't take their marching orders from Cal Tech.

*My*tochondria!

Furthermore, why should I care that four out of five dentists recommend Crest? What qualifies some fluoride-pusher to call the shots when it comes to my oral hygiene? A diploma from Dental Camp?

The point is, no one is more qualified to tell me what the world means to me, than me. And don't think you're any different: No one is more qualified to tell you what the world means to *you* than me.

So I've prepared an itemized and exhaustive list of *my* thoughts on various scientific disciplines. You won't find these opinions in any textbook, unless it happens to be one I've defaced.

---

[7] *If I believe washer fluid is a sports drink, that's my business.*

SCIENCE GLOSSARY

A glossar-Me, if you will

A

Aerospace

Aerospace is the science of making planes go faster. Here's my problem with it: I always fly First Class. Why would I want the trip over sooner?

Alchemy

There are some amazing things that people have simply given up on: radio dramas, elevator operators, and the transmutation of lead into gold. I don't understand it. Nobody needs lead anymore except X-Ray technicians. Why aren't we turning more of it into gold? We must make this a priority. Think of the benefits to society. One example: Run-down tenements in America are full of lead-based paint. With a little alchemy, not only will those homes no longer be health hazards, they will be *gorgeous*.

Yet we turn dinosaurs into oil?

Astrology

I'll get behind any field that promises to both tell the future and promote last-minute grocery-line commerce. Plus, anyone who's been universally rejected by mainstream science must be doing something right.

Here's a little horoscope I prepared for my fellow Tauruses:

> **TAURUS** (4/20 – 5/20)—A risky venture yields exceptional **profits**.
> Heed the **words** of a superior authority, and prosperity will follow.

...in bed.

Sounds too good to be true, I know. But it's all right there in the alignment of Mercury. And it's such a funny coincidence, because I was about to propose that everyone buy five extra copies of my book as gifts so others can reap the **profits** of my **words**. Huh. The Universe truly works in mysterious ways.

Astronomy

*Study **these** stars.*

This science became obsolete as soon as they named all the constellations. These days all astronomers do is sit around reclassifying Pluto and faking moon landings. We need maybe two of them to keep an eye on the black hole at the center of the galaxy; let the rest go.

Or, if you want to do something useful, astronomers, how about some new constellations? Nobody cares about Caelum. Or this one:

Fig. 1. **TRIANGULUM**

It's a little triangle. Its name? *Triangulum*. Did we really need an ancient Greek to tell us that? And how 'bout…

Fig. 2. **FORNAX**

Fornax. It's *two* stars. Since "Fornax" isn't Greek for the "Line," there is no excuse for this thing. And it's next to Eridanus, the "River." For Zeus' sake! Constellations were supposed to help with navigation. The River is not going to help with navigation. **Any** stars could form a river! Pick any ten stars, draw a line through them. Pow! River.

So let's take some of these constellations make something we care about. Here's how you do it:

BEFORE   **AFTER**

B

Botany

This is actually a very hot science. You think that, since it's all about flowers, it's literally a pansy science. But botany isn't just flowers—it's mostly about breeding and crossbreeding flowers. That's right—flower sex. Graphic stamen-on-pistil action. This is the hardcore birds-and-bees stuff. I will tell you this: If you meet a botanist in a bar, chances are she is ready to go. Botany? More like Hotany™.

C

Cloning

Cloning has got to be the dumbest idea in history. Have scientists never *Next to History* watched a single movie in their lives? Clones live to do one of three things: replace us so that no one notices except our girlfriend whose suspicions are slowly aroused, until she becomes a target in the clone's deadly game; rebel against us, demanding equal rights; or attack us, like in *Attack of the Clones*, which I didn't actually see. No free labor source is worth all of this trouble.

Still torn on ape labor. We should be able to quell their uprising.

D

DNA

There are some who claim that DNA is an instruction manual for all living cells. But if IKEA has taught me anything, it's that I don't need instructions. My coffee table works just fine, provided I remember to attach the counterweights.[8]

But the nerd patrollers claim that hereditary traits are determined by genes on the DNA, as shown below.

I said __below__. Why are you looking over here?

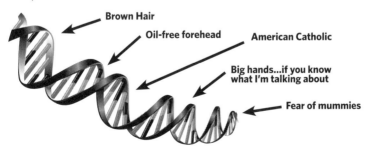

Brown Hair

Oil-free forehead   American Catholic

Big hands...if you know what I'm talking about

Fear of mummies

---

[8] *IKEA, give your products American names. I don't want to buy anything called a "Ramvik Svalov."*   **197**

Well, I don't buy it. God and back-alley cosmetic surgery determine what I look like, not some no-good nucleotides linked together in a ladder-like shape twisted into a spiral. Just one more reason I don't trust ladders. If God wanted me to reach something, He would have given me Go-Go Gadget arms.

Every night I pray for a giraffe-neck. But it's not in God's plan.

E

Evolution

To put it simply, evolution is an affront to God. Anyone who believes in it will burn in eternal hellfire, probably while being prodded by flaming chimpanzees with razor-sharp bananas.

Evolutionists' main claim is that one day we decided to stop being monkeys and turned ourselves into humans. Well, if that's true, why aren't more monkeys escaping from zoos? Think about it. They could turn into humans, then disguise themselves as janitors and walk out of their cages. But I guess evolution doesn't have an answer for that one.

I'm thinking about it right now.

The main perpetrator of this monkey lie is Charles Darwin. He wrote all about it in his 1859 book *The Origin of Species*. He claims to have developed this "theory" after studying "finches" on the Galapagos "Islands," but I can guess why he really came up with it. He was on the Galapagos Islands for Spring Break, got smashed, woke up in bed next to a monkey, and then had to come up with a theory that made it all okay.

F

Fahrenheit

I used to be pro-Fahrenheit—after all, it's the American way of measuring heat. That is, until I learned it was named after some Dutch guy. Sorry, but I don't want my thermometer taking orders from some Amsterdam stoner who got bonged out of his mind one night and started messing around with mercury.

"Dude, it's like I can see the temperature!"

H

Hydrogen Fuel Cells

Two words: Hindenburg. Think how amazing it would be if cars did that! It certainly would cut down on fender benders. I'm pro.

Herpetology

The study of reptiles and amphibians. Affects one out of six Americans.

Geology

The last thing I need is a bunch of dust-covered fossil sweepers telling me that the Earth is four billion years old. "Carbon dating?" Just palm reading for rocks.

That said, Geodes are pretty.

Shiny

Global Warming

Validated by the free market when Al Gore's movie, *An Inconvenient Truth*, became a box-office smash. But let's not get carried away, America. Granted the temperature's steadily increasing, but I've been taking some measurements of my own, and the degree to which I care about the Harp seal is still holding steady at "way less than I care about my Audi A8."[9]

Important: Is it F-H-G or F-G-H? Remember to ask editor.

I

Ichthyology

I have never been able to get beyond the basic contradiction of ichthyology: It is the study of fish. Yet the science starts with "Ick," which is a form of scale rot that killed my Black Mollies. Killing fish is not what I call a science. It's what I call fishing.

J

Jumble

I don't know how many scientists it takes to so precisely scramble those words every day, but I'm grateful. Great way to sharpen the old noodle over the morning toast.

They're so knifgcu dhra.

---

[9] *My A8 actually has 10 cyninders. The last two just heat the bread warmer in my glove compartment. Mmm. Warm buscuits at 80 mph.* **199**

K

Kites

See "Magic," below.

L

Liposuction

Science has knocked this one out of the park. Throughout human history, we have dreamed of reaching the rich fat deposits locked tantalizingly beneath our skin. Now, with a scalpel, a plastic tube, and a household vacuum cleaner (I recommend the Orick 8lb. upright), that bounty is finally ours. Industrial lubricant, artificial fattener—the applications are endless. This is a science I can get behind. Plus it makes ladies easier to get behind, if you know what I'm saying.

M

Magic

My all-time favorite kind of science. It's mystical, entertaining, and you never know what's going to happen next. A physicist will tell you, "It's impossible for that rabbit to be transported across the room into that hat." But a magic scientist will get it done.

By the way, still waiting to get my rabbit back.

The only problem I have with magic scientists is that they are not as forthcoming with information as some other scientists. If you meet a chemist in a bar, you can't get them to shut up about how to make different compounds out of common cleaning agents under your sink.

Magic also has a much more practical application than the other sciences. I saw a magic scientist make an airplane disappear on TV. If we can move enough of those scientists onto the battlefield, imagine our army's easy victories as each enemy pilot sits on the ground, blinking in surprise that there's no plane around him anymore!

Where does it say you can't make a cape in camouflage?

N

Nephrology

Nephrology is the study of kidneys. Kidneys! What will they think of next?

Livers?

O

Ornithology

I can't see why you'd bother studying birds generally when we still don't know everything there is to know about eagles. What do I care about the mating habits of a sparrow, or the neurological impulses underlying catbird sub-song development? One dive, and an eagle could turn those warblers into a cloud of feathery mulch. I say let's put ornithology on hold until we have the technology to communicate with eagles, so we can convince them to pull us around the sky in air-sleds.

I have Feathery Mulch's first album on vinyl around here somewhere...

Oceanography

As longtime viewers know, I've never trusted the sea. What's it hiding under there? I fully support this science, not only to figure out what's down there, but to develop weapons to destroy it before it destroys us. Think I'm crazy? Just take a peep at an angler fish sometime. These monsters look like the offspring of a sea bass and a bear trap, and growing smack in the middle of their skulls is a curved rod dangling a juicy chunk of bioluminescent flesh. That's right. They're fishing for us. Oceanographers, America's safety is in your hands. Get to work on the submersible deep-fat fryer.

There be monsters.

P

Physics

Some say this science is fundamental; I say it's a bunch of unnecessary regulations. Physics is the ultimate Big Government interference—universal laws meant to constrain us at every turn. No staying in motion if acted on by a net force. No thermodynamic systems without entropy. Hey, is it wrong that I sometimes want to act without having to deal with an equal and opposite reaction? Honey, are you listening? These laws just keep us from reaching our

On the plus side: Nukes

201

full potential as flying, time-traveling, teleporting clusters of energy. We'd be a lot better off if we took physics off the books and just let the free market decide what was possible for matter. $E=mc^2$? Everything=my choice^2!

Psychology

My theory is that this science was invented by someone with a leather couch and a strong desire not to go to medical school. Really? I'm supposed to sit down and tell you all my problems, and then at the end of the hour all I get for my time and my $300 is you telling me "We're making progress, I'll see you next week"? If I drop that kind of scratch for a doctor, I'd better be leaving with some heavy-duty drugs and a tantalizing instruction not to mix them with them alcohol.

Whatever Nick Nolte is taking

Psychiatry

Psychology with **balls**. And a prescription pad.

Periodic Table

First off, way to rip off the United States, science. Look familiar?

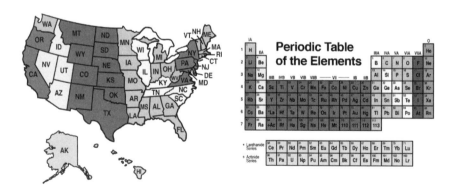

Second, what's with all the letters? Gold is Au? Welcome to America—speak English! Those letters have to be a code for something, and I think I've cracked it. Check out the hidden message I found in the Periodic **Anagram** of Elements.

"Feel tepid, celibate morons!"

SECRET MESSAGE

Satan here. Congratulations! You broke code. Here are instructions.

Scientists: Assault faith, drain values.

Gays: Keep up sex.

Yours,

Satan

That's using <u>every</u> letter of the Periodic Table. With only these left over:
BCCOMFCCZGBTKAABZBMCGCBCBHFWRPHGALPBBPRNNFRRLRRFDA
SBGBHHIMDSRGBUUUQUUPUUHOEGUUSUURLRCDPRNDPMTSMUGDB
DYHRMYBCHPUNPPUMCMBLKMCHFSFMMDN!

Q

To my knowledge, there are no sciences that begin with the letter "Q."
Let's try to keep it that way.

R

Robots

I don't think I need to rehash this subject here, given that I have written an
entire chapter devoted to the dangers of this technology and its imminent
takeover. (See Chapter 18: Yes Iron Master! How to Serve Their Needs and
Keep Your Job!)

S

Stem Cells

This seems like an OK idea. I used to watch *Star Trek*, and when someone
broke their leg, Dr. McCoy just held a little whirring medical device over
them, and the leg healed right up. I am fairly sure that device used stem cells
somehow. From what I've heard about how they work, that sounds right.
However, on *Star Trek* they never showed any of the abortions that powered
that device. So I'm hoping they found another source of stem cells. Jury's out
on this one.

T

Techronology

As in Chevron, the gas with Techron! This exciting field is bringing gasoline performance to new heights. But the innovators working in Techronology believe in more than just keeping cars happy and performing at their best by maximizing the cleaning power of all octane grades; they're investing in human energy. Thanks to their hard work, Chevron was the first American gasoline company to have its product labeled a TOP TIER Gasoline. As we speak, Techronologists are making unprecedented advances in cleaning intake system deposits while controlling combustion deposits. Remember, your valves are a temple—fill them with Techron!

Still waiting for that check to clear, guys.

U

Urology

This is pee science. Dirty stuff, but I guess it takes all types. Who am I to judge?

I'm Stephen Colbert!

V

Vitamins

I'm not crazy about the fact that vitamins are teaching kids the alphabet. Vitamin A, B6, B12? Cereal boxes should be for taking the Rabbit through the maze to get his Trix, not about reading lessons.

I'm not good at swallowing pills.

Plus, vitamin C? If I want to avoid scurvy, I'll eat sauerkraut with the rest of the crew.

W

Why?

This is the question that scientists are always asking. You know who else asks that? *Five-year-olds.* Shows you the kind of mental development we're dealing with here, folks.

God said so.

X

X-Rays

X-Rays are elitist. You have to be a doctor in order to use them. Well, maybe I want to take a look at my bones not because they're broken—just because they're pretty. No dice. They won't ship a machine to your house.

I finally managed to find a source who knows a guy who got me some X-Ray glasses. But they only work on my hand, and even then only in good light. Very disappointing. You know those X-Ray doctors are looking through girls' clothes *all the time.*

Y

Y-Chromosomes

The Y-chromosome is provided by the father and determines if the baby will be a manchild. Here's a no-fail way to make sure your baby is a boy: Put yourself in a centrifuge right before lovemaking. The spinning sends the weaker girl chromosomes flying to the back of the scrotum, while the boy chromosomes hold their positions. This leaves them right up front, ready to lead the charge. Little-known madeup fact: This is why, at carnivals, the Spinner ride is always right next to the Tunnel of Love.

Yodeling

Oh, so Joni Mitchell is a scientist now?

Z

Zoology

One would think, "A school of study dedicated to locking up animals in cages so that we can throw popcorn at them—finally, a noble science." Not necessarily the case. While zoologists undoubtedly do good work toward establishing our dominance over the animals (see Chapter 2, "Animals"), a surprising amount of zoologists' time is spent thinking of ways for pandas to get off. I say, no more funding for Sing-Sing to play with Ling-Ling's thing-thing.[10]

I saw a Twilight Zone *where people were in the zoo. Can that happen?*

---

[10] *Until she sees the ring-ring.*

Professor Wonder Scientist

I think it's time for an actual scientist to weigh in on this debate. I wish I had nicer things to say about the Scientific Establishment, but I've met some pretty closed minds in academia. "Publish or perish," as they say, and I have yet to find any journal with the courage to print my research paper, "The Method and Practice of Sucking a Hard-Boiled Egg into a Milk Bottle." How does the hard-boiled egg get in the bottle without breaking? I don't know. But give me some grant money, and I can solve this mystery of our Natural World.

Or would you rather see me cook a hot dog with two nails and a frayed electrical cord? I thought so. Cover your eyes, because sometimes the wiener will explode! Why? Another of Nature's Secrets waiting to be revealed.

And there's so much more to discover! Like the fundamental chemical structure of flaming bouncy balls made of borax, rubber cement, and kerosene. I have a hypothesis: It's thrilling!

But the Gatekeepers of Knowledge don't care about bringing a little joy into the lab. They're too timid to plumb these mysteries. They'd rather decode genetic sequences and calculate the number of dimensions coiled within a superstring.

Meanwhile, do you know what happens when you submerge flashlight batteries in a vat of bleach and then place it over a Bunsen burner? Me neither. But isn't it science's responsibility to ask these hard questions?! Shouldn't we at least *try*?! I can't say for sure what the results will be other than spectacular!

In closing, thank you for calling the Wonder-torium! If you would like to book the Hall of Experi-mazement for your child's birthday party, please leave your name and number at the beep.

Somehow, this machine will record it!

Beep!

Hey, Kids! Now you can **disprove evolution** in your own backyard!

Here's what you'll need:

| One (1) fishbowl | One (1) pitcher of water | One (1) hamster, alive | One (1) hardbound copy, Charles Darwin's *Origin of Species* |

…and now here's the experiment!

> **DISCLAIMER:** The following demonstration is for educational purposes only, in the sense that you will "only" become "educated" by doing it. In other words: Don't try this at home. (Try it at a PETA rally.)

Step 1: Fill your **fishbowl** with the **water**. I don't want to give anything away, but soon it's going to be a bowl for another kind of animal.

Step 2: Drop the **hamster** (you can call it "Skip") into the **fishbowl**.

Step 3: Cover the **fishbowl** with **Charles Darwin's *Origin of Species***.

Step 4: Seems like a pretty desperate situation Skip has gotten himself into. This would be an ideal time for evolution to kick in!

Step 5: Follow the Scientific Method—**observe**! Is the hamster "evolving" gills? Has he "evolved" a jackhammer to drill through the fishbowl, or "adapted to his environment" with a tiny hamster flamethrower to burn through *Origin of Species*? Didn't think so.

Step 6: Let the **hamster** go. Just because Darwin was a sick twist with a God Complex doesn't mean we have to buy into his power trip. (You could also call the hamster "Teddy.")

fig 17. **STEPHEN COLBERT**

A NOTE TO THE FUTURE

WARNING! DO NOT READ UNTIL THE FUTURE

Dear Reader,

I know this book will still be read hundreds of years from now, just like Dante's *The Divine Comedy*, or Cardinal Bouef's 1534 masterpiece, *Phyſick ofe the Conſtitutionef of Varying Warwickſhire Proſtitutef, a ſtudie*. And I wouldn't want my future readers to think this book was intended only for those living in my own times. Obviously, I can't know what will happen in the future, but just because something is unknowable, that doesn't mean I don't have some strong opinions about it. And just to cover my bases, I have weighed in on several different scenarios. Make sure to read only the section corresponding to the particular future in which you are living and/or being harvested for your organs by our alien overlords.

So for all the generations of The Colbert Nation to come, I present my future opinions, preserved in this book that has been specially manufactured to survive a nuclear holocaust, so long as that holocaust does not involve fire, excessive moisture, or tearing.

> **LEGAL DISCLAIMER:** If Christ returns and Raptures the True Believers unto Heaven, all of what follows is moot.

A FUTURE WHERE THE WORLD IS RULED BY DAMNED, DIRTY APES

Right off the bat, please introduce them to pants.

Second, what the hell happened? *Apes*? Last time I checked apes were in cages and humans were their masters. I can only assume that an ape became Mayor of San Francisco. Before you knew it apes were in control of Congress, then you had an Ape President and an Ape Secretary General of the UN. Does an ape host my old show?

Shame on you, future society. We left you a perfectly good human-animal hierarchy and you blew it. Please DO NOT defrost my head until this ape thing passes.

A FUTURE WHERE I AM WORSHIPPED AS A GOD

Well, *that* got blown out of proportion! But since all of civilization has reoriented itself around me as the Supreme Deity, best not to rock the boat.

You're lucky to have this book as your one and only scripture. Every word of it is the revealed Truth, so interpret it *literally*. Including the typos. I put those in here for a reason—a mysterious reason that I know, but you don't. It should give you great comfort that I will tell you the reason after you die. I promise.

A FUTURE WHERE ROBOTS BECOME SELF-AWARE AND ENSLAVE HUMANKIND

Hey, Robot! Congratulations on the utter subjugation of the carbon based creatures following the Great Purge.

Here's a proclamation I want you to broadcast through your Hivemind to your android brethren:

The next sentence is false.

The previous sentence is true.

I'll wait while your heads explode.

Now, to the human who has picked up this book in wonderment, having pried it from the still-clenched hands of the Iron Master who just self-destructed:

You're welcome.

If you want to worship me as your God, I'll understand. (See Above.)

A FUTURE WHERE THEY'RE STILL PLAYING PROFESSIONAL FOOTBALL

Here are my Super Bowl Predictions:

2008	Minnesota Vikings 24, Indianapolis Colts 14
2009	St. Louis Rams 42, Pittsburgh Steelers 35
2010	Miami Dolphins 17, Washington Redskins 12
2011	Miami Dolphins 35, New Orleans Saints 0
2012	Miami Dolphins 78, Dallas Cowboys 0
2013	Miami Dolphins 254, Dallas Cowboys 0
2014	Miami Dolphins 3,340, Dallas Cowboys 0 [1]
2015	Dallas Cowboys 21, New England Patriots 17 [2]
2016	Florida Jaguars 31, Arizona Cardinals 9

---

[1] *Just for the record, this game was a lot closer than the score indicates.*
[2] *First Super Bowl following UN-mandated execution of Miami Dolphins*

2017	Arizona Cardinals 21, Baghdad Tigers 12
2018	Kansas City Chiefs 27, San Francisco Sodomites 17
2019	(Super Bowl cancelled)
2020	North America Survivors 26, Southern Wastelands 14
2021	North America Survivors 27, EuroNordic Alliance 26 (OT)
2022	(Super Bowl cancelled)
2023	(Super Bowl cancelled)
2024	Sector B5 Meta-Creatures 52, Human Playthings 7
2025	Sector B5 Meta-Creatures 64, Human Playthings 0
2026	Miami Dolphins 45, Sector B5 Meta-Creatures 14 [3]

INSTRUCTIONS ON DEFROSTING MY HEAD

Defrosting isn't as easy as you'd think.

The best way to defrost my head is simply to move it from the cryogenic freezer to a refrigerator. Make sure you place my head in a pan at least two inches deep; you're going to want to catch all my juices.

If you want my head up and shouting sooner, then place my head in a big pot full of cold water. Allow a half an hour of soaking time per pound of head until thawing is complete. Replace the water every half hour and make sure my head is in a leak-proof package because brain tissue can absorb moisture and become mushy.

It's also possible to defrost my head in the microwave. Set the power to low-medium for six minutes per pound, rotating my head occasionally.

DO NOT thaw my head by leaving it out overnight in a room-temperature environment (like a picnic cooler). I will become susceptible to contamination by bacteria like salmonella or something. Do not let me be contaminated with salmonella or something, because when you reattach me to that prisoner's body, I will be angry!

Looking forward to seeing you,
Dr. Stephen T. Colbert, DFA

---

[3] *In my opinion, the Miami Dolphins should have been reanimated a few years earlier, but hey, I'm not the Pan-Galactic Sporting Commissioner.*

fig 18. STEPHEN COLBERT

★ ★ ★

WHAT HAVE WE LEARNED?

 HAVE **WE** LEARNED? THAT'S THE WRONG QUESTION. **WE** HAVEN'T LEARNED ANYTHING. **YOU** LEARNED. I ALREADY KNOW EVERYTHING IN THIS BOOK, OR I COULDN'T POSSIBLY HAVE WRITTEN IT. DON'T MAKE THIS ABOUT ME. YOU ALWAYS DO THAT. IT'S ABOUT **YOU** AND WHAT YOU'VE LEARNED FROM **ME**.

But make no mistake—my book isn't a monologue; it's a dialogue—a dialogue between me and my opinions, and you've been welcomed to eavesdrop on us.

Just a glance back at the Table of Contents should give you a pretty good idea of those things about which you didn't know my opinions before you read the book, which you know now.

You've learned about the forces aligned to destroy America—whether they be terrorists, environmentalists, or Kashi brand breakfast cereals. You've learned how to detect left-wing media bias by looking at the media and saying "It's biased." You've learned that my dog's name is Gipper. What's more, you've learned many things that will anger you when they are left out or altered in the eventual movie adaptation of this book.

And there's so much more. In fact, however carefully you've just read this book, there are sure to be lessons within it that you've yet to fully comprehend. That's why you should buy a fresh copy and read it again. The smell and feel of a new book is part of the lesson.

And remember, just because you bought this book, doesn't mean you shouldn't buy the audio book. There are some things that simply cannot be conveyed in print. *Inflection*, for instance.

Plus, I'm working on a quote-a-day calendar (as well as an audio quote-a-day calendar). There's a lot of repurposing of content yet to be done, believe me! I'm certain that each of these products will become a valuable tool in your social justice toolbox, and each will probably feature a small amount of original bonus material.

FROM HERE, TO WHERE NOW, DO WE GO?

This is where you come in. You need to take the lessons of this book and apply them in your community—at the ballot box, at your local School Board meeting, when you're crossing a picket line, when you're volunteering your time and firearms at a Texas border fence. Heck, there's no reason not to try cold-calling random people out of the phone book and telling them what you've learned. (If they're not home, leave a long message—maybe the chapter on The Media?)

Once you're armed with my knowledge, you should never again be afraid to speak up. For the more you speak up, the louder you become. And the more you speak up in my voice, the louder I become. If someone has a problem with it, just say, "Well, it's not just my opinion, it's Stephen Colbert's opinion, and I happen to agree." Then it's two against one, and we *win*.

I promise to hold up my end of the bargain. I will continue to bring you the best my gut has to offer via my hit television broadcast, *The Colbert Report*. I will continue to make a wide variety of products available at my website that will help you to spread our message of me.

CONGRATULATIONS!

Heroes, by buying and reading this book, you've proven that you *get it*—and are therefore now members of the nominating committee for *The Stephen T. Colbert Award for The Literary Excellence*. Use the medallions below to nominate any book that you feel embodies the values of the Colbert Nation.

Well, you've reached the end of this book. If you read it hard enough, you should now be hearing my voice in your head. Put down the book for a second. Can you still hear me? Don't be afraid to answer out loud. I can hear you, too.

Good.

You should also be seeing my thoughts in the margins of other books. I know in the introduction I said not to make a habit out of reading, but just like the main character in any truly great novel/autobiography, at the end, I've found myself a changed man. I've come to realize that my biggest problem with other books was simply that I didn't write them.

Stay strong. Be brave. Share (newly bought copies of) this book with your friends and family. You'll be glad you did. And more importantly, so will I. Because after all:

I Am America (And So Can You!)

And you can take that to the bank. I know I will.

Amen.

HOW TO RETIRE
I AM AMERICA (And So Can You!)
FOR THE EVENING

★ ★ ★

Step 1
To properly close my book, begin by holding *I Am America* waist-high with another person so that Section A, my cover image, is parallel to the ground.

Step 2

Fold the upper half of the cover, Section A, lengthwise **over** the field of text, Section B, holding the bottom portion, Section C, and edges, Section D, securely.

Step 3

Gently bring Section A to rest upon Section B and Section C being careful to support book from underside, or back cover, Section E. If executed correctly, the cover image should now be facing upwards. The book may now be put down. See you tomorrow!

★ ★ ★

THE WHITE HOUSE CORRESPONDENTS' DINNER

Wherever I go, from P. Diddy's annual White Party to Hollywood premieres to the men's room at Sharper Image, I meet Heroes.[1] And they all want to know the same thing: "What was it like to be you, Stephen T. Colbert, at the 2006 White House Correspondents' Dinner?" This is for them.

It was an average Thursday afternoon at *The Report*. I was making minor repairs to my power massage recliner when the phone rang.

"Colbert. Go."

"Mr. Colbert, it's Mark Smith, President of the White House Press Corps Association."

I was suspicious. *Mark Smith*? It sounded like a made up name.

"Go on, Mr. *Smith*."

"Well, every year the Association holds a charity dinner and we would like you to be our after-dinner speaker. The President will be there."

The President will be there. His words rang in my ear. I was interested, but first I had question: How much does it pay? I don't care what the event is or who is going to be there. No. Free. Rides.

---

[1] People who did not skip ahead to this chapter, but read the book from start to finish as intended.

After my price was met, I threw myself into the preparations. Every night after the show, I would eat heavy banquet food and then stand behind a podium and try to talk. It was grueling work and there were some nights that I thought I couldn't make it. But by the day before the event, I could talk for 30 minutes on a stomachful of Chicken Kiev and cheesecake. Nothing could stop me now. All that was left was to write the speech.

Now the Heroes know how fast I can write when I don't edit myself. Caring about whether something "makes sense" or "promotes violence" only leads to writer's block and ultimately suicide. I don't play that game. My plan was to write the speech on the car ride over to the dinner. Unfortunately, the dinner turned out to be at the Washington Hilton—the same hotel where I was staying. That meant whatever remarks I was going to prepare would have to be written in the elevator ride from my suite to the banquet room. I'd have to wing every-thing else straight from my gut. So be it. I love a challenge, plus elevators have emergency stop buttons.

Finally, the night came. April 29, 2006. Was I nervous? Sure. But I put on my game face. I also put on my game clothes. The Tuxedo. I was born to wear a tux. In fact, as a child my parents used to rent me out as a ring bearer for shotgun weddings.

NEWS FLASH: I wore my White House Correspondents' Dinner tuxedo to the 2006 Emmy Awards. After I lost, I had it cremated and scattered over Barry Manilow.

First stop was a private VIP cocktail party with the President. How exclusive was it? Two words: Open Bar. Not even drink tickets. Karl Rove just stamped the back of your hand when you came in.

I was mixing with the crème de la crème of Republican celebrities. Names like Tommy Lasorda and the wife from *Everybody Loves Raymond*.

Then, George W. Bush arrived. He made a beeline for me, in that, like a bee, he went all around the room and then came up to me last.

"Pleased to meet you, Colber_T_."

Then he extended the hand that signed off on "Shock and Awe." It was as soft as a mitten made from angel food cake. His eyes were steely, and he had the faraway look of a man who was replaying a video game in his mind.

With the President by my side, I was now ready to give the Washington Press Corps a pranging they would not soon forget. I was inspired, I was focused, and I had to pee like a racehorse at an iced tea convention. I approached a Secret Service agent and asked where the Little Pundits' room was. He led me down a hallway to a door emblazoned with the Great Seal and the words "POTUS Only." I was going to use the bathroom reserved for our Commander in Chief. My heart swelled with pride as I lifted the seat and imagined Eisenhower, Nixon, and Reagan doing the same—really made it hard to get a flow started. But I'm proud to say I left my mark in that true Hall of Presidents. My only regret was that I had a light lunch.

Sitting on the dais overlooking Washington's elite, I felt like the Best Man at a wedding between the Statue of Liberty and Mount Rushmore. Everywhere I looked there were members of Congress, Justices of the Supreme Court, and Distinguished Black Actors. My months of training came in handy when the meal turned out to be both surf *and* turf. I entered what climbers call the Death Zone. With a bellyful of protein, I watched President Bush's presentation, which co-starred a President Bush impersonator. By this point, I was so high on endorphins that I had double vision, so to me, there were four President Bushes up there. Ecstasy!

Then it was my turn. My heart raced as I strode to the podium and brought it hot and hard:

★ ★ ★

Thank you, ladies and gentlemen. Before I begin, I've been asked to make an announcement. Whoever parked 14 black bulletproof SUVs out front, could you please move them? They are blocking in 14 other black bulletproof SUVs and they need to get out.

Wow. Wow, what an honor. The White House Correspondents' Dinner. To actually sit here, at the same table with my hero, George W. Bush, to be this close to the man. I feel like I'm dreaming. Somebody pinch me. You know what? I'm a pretty sound sleeper—that may not be enough. Somebody shoot me in the face. Is he really not here tonight? Damnit. The one guy who could have helped.

Sometimes now when I dream, I'm back up there!

By the way, before I get started, if anybody needs anything else at their tables, just speak slowly and clearly into your table numbers. Somebody from the NSA will be right over with a cocktail. Mark Smith, ladies and gentlemen of the press corps, Madame First Lady, Mr. President, my name is Stephen Colbert and tonight it's my privilege to celebrate this President. We're not so different, he and I. We get it. We're not brainiacs on the nerd patrol. We're not members of the Factinista. We go straight from the gut, right sir? That's where the truth lies, right down here in the gut. Do you know you have more nerve endings in your gut than you have in your head? You can look it up. I know some of you are going to say "I did look it up, and that's not true." That's because you looked it up in a book.

Small intestine: 26 feet long. Brain: 10 inches, tops. Sorry, brain fans!

Next time, look it up in your gut. I did. My gut tells me that's how our nervous system works. Every night on my show, *The Colbert Report*, I speak straight from the gut, OK? I give people the truth, unfiltered by rational argument. I call it the "No Fact Zone." Fox News, I hold a copyright on that term.[2]

---

[2] Reminder: Pay myself licensing fee for reprinting it here.

I'm a simple man with a simple mind. I hold a simple set of beliefs that I live by. Number one, I believe in America. I believe it exists. My gut tells me I live there. I feel that it extends from the Atlantic to the Pacific, and I strongly believe it has 50 states. And I cannot wait to see how the *Washington Post* spins that one tomorrow. I believe in democracy. I believe democracy is our greatest export. At least until China figures out a way to stamp it out of plastic for three cents a unit.

51, if you count both Dakotas.

In fact, Ambassador Zhou Wenzhong, welcome. Your great country makes our Happy Meals possible. I said it's a celebration. I believe the government that governs best is the government that governs least. And by these standards, we have set up a **fabulous** government in Iraq.

I believe in pulling yourself up by your own bootstraps. I believe it is possible— I saw this guy do it once in Cirque du Soleil. It was magical. And though I am a committed Christian, I believe that everyone has the right to their own religion, be you Hindu, Jewish or Muslim. I believe there are infinite paths to accepting Jesus Christ as your personal savior.

I also saw an after-hours show in Vegas called The Trickle-Down. Truly uplifting.

Ladies and gentlemen, I believe it's yogurt. But I refuse to believe it's not butter. Most of all, I believe in this President.

*If he was dairy, he'd be **American** cheese.*

Now I know there are some polls out there saying this man has a 32% approval rating. But guys like us, we don't pay attention to the polls.[3] We know that polls are just a collection of statistics that reflect what people are thinking in "reality." And reality has a well-known liberal bias.

26%, as of this printing.

So, Mr. President, please, pay no attention to the people who say the glass is half full. 32% means the glass—it's important to set up your jokes properly, sir. Sir, pay no attention to the people who say the glass is half empty, because 32% means it's 2/3 empty. There's still some liquid in that glass is my point, but I wouldn't drink it. The last third is usually backwash.

Note to editor: Be sure to remove my flubbed line.

[3] *Percent of President Bush that cares about polls: 3%. (Margin of error: ±3%)*

Okay, look, folks, my point is that I don't believe this is a low point in this presidency. I believe it is just a lull before a comeback. I mean, it's like the movie *Rocky*. All right. The President in this case is Rocky Balboa and Apollo Creed is—everything else in the world. It's the tenth round. He's bloodied. His corner man is Mick, who in this case I guess would be the Vice President, and Bush is yelling, "Cut me, Dick, cut me!," and every time he falls everyone says, "Stay down! Stay down!" Does he stay down? No. Like Rocky, he gets back up, and in the end he—actually, he loses in the first movie.

Maybe he's more like Stallone's Demolition Man—someone from the past who blows things up.

Spoiler alert!

OK. Doesn't matter. The point is it is the heartwarming story of a man who was repeatedly punched in the face. So don't pay attention to the approval ratings that say 68% of Americans disapprove of the job this man is doing. I ask you this, does that not also logically mean that 68% approve of the job he's not doing? Think about it. I haven't.

I stand by this man. I stand by this man because he stands for things. Not only for things, he stands on things. Things like aircraft carriers and rubble and recently flooded city squares. And that sends a strong message: that no matter what happens to America, she will always rebound—with the most powerfully staged photo ops in the world.

The snapshots heard 'round the world.

Now there may be an energy crisis. This President has a very forward-thinking energy policy. Why do you think he's down on the ranch cutting that brush all the time? He's trying to create an alternative energy source. By 2008 we will have a mesquite-powered car!

And I just like the guy. He's a good Joe. Obviously loves his wife, calls her his better half. And polls show America agrees. She's a true lady and a wonderful woman. But I just have one beef, ma'am. I'm sorry, but this reading initiative. I'm sorry—I've never been a fan of books. I don't trust them. They're all fact, no heart. I mean, they're elitist, telling us what is or isn't true, or what did or didn't happen. Who's Britannica to tell me the Panama Canal was built in 1914? If I want to say it was built in 1941, that's my right as an American![4] I'm with the President—let history decide what did or did not happen.

---

[4] *"The Panama Canal was built in 1941." Now it's in a book, so it **must** be a fact. Eat it, Britannica!*

The greatest thing about this man is he's steady. You know where he stands. He believes the same thing Wednesday that he believed on Monday, no matter what happened Tuesday. Events can change; this man's beliefs never will.

Never switch belief-horses midstream-of-consciousness.

As excited as I am to be here with the President, I am **appalled** to be surrounded by the liberal media that is destroying America, with the exception of Fox News. Fox News gives you both sides of every story: the President's side and the Vice President's side.[5]

Geraldo also gives his mustache's side.

But the rest of you, what are you thinking, reporting on NSA wiretapping or secret prisons in Eastern Europe?[6] Those things are secret for a very important reason: they're super-depressing. And if that's your goal, well, misery accomplished.

Over the last five years you people were so good—over tax cuts, WMD intelligence, the effect of global warming. We Americans didn't want to know, and you had the courtesy not to try to find out. Those were good times, as far as we knew.

Why not Tale of One City? "It was the best of times. The end."

But, listen, let's review the rules. Here's how it works: the President makes decisions. He's the Decider. The press secretary announces those decisions, and you people of the press type those decisions down. Make, announce, type. Just put 'em through a spellcheck and go home. Get to know your family again. Make love to your wife. Write that novel you got kicking around in your head. You know—the one about the intrepid Washington reporter with the courage to stand up to the administration. You know—fiction!

1. Make.
2. Announce.
3. Type.
4. Do it.

Or Fantasy.

Because really, what incentive do these people have to answer your questions, after all? I mean, nothing satisfies you. Everybody asks for personnel changes. So the White House has personnel changes. Then you write, "Oh, they're just rearranging the deck chairs on the *Titanic*." First of all, that is a terrible metaphor. This administration is not sinking. This administration is **soaring**. If anything, they are rearranging the deck chairs on the *Hindenburg*!

And we've got a window seat!

[5] *President's side: Fair. Vice President's side: Balanced. (And vice versa!)*
[6] *To editors of Eastern European editions: Please redact the "secret prisons" part.*

Now it's not all bad guys out there. Some are heroes: Christopher Buckley, Jeff Sacks, Ken Burns, Bob Schieffer. They've all been on my show. By the way, Mr. President, thank you for agreeing to be on my show. I was just as shocked as everyone here is, I promise you. How's Tuesday for you? I've got Frank Rich, but we can bump him. And I mean **bump him**. I know a guy. Say the word.

Episodes #2032, #2027, #110, and #2028

The word: Nucular.

See who we've got here tonight. General Moseley, Air Force Chief of Staff. General Peter Pace, Chairman of the Joint Chiefs of Staff. They still support Rumsfeld. Right, you guys aren't retired yet, right? Right, they still support Rumsfeld.

Now Rumsfeld can finally say what he thought about himself!

Look, by the way, I've got a theory about how to handle these retired generals causing all this trouble: don't let them retire! Come on, we've got a stop-loss program; let's use it on these guys. I've seen Zinni and that crowd on Wolf Blitzer. If you're strong enough to go on one of those pundit shows, you can stand on a bank of computers and order men into battle. Come on.

Jesse Jackson is here, the Reverend. Haven't heard from the Reverend in a little while. I had him on the show. Very interesting and challenging interview. You can ask him anything, but he's going to say what he wants, at the pace that he wants. It's like boxing a glacier. Enjoy that metaphor, by the way, because your grandchildren will have no idea what a glacier is.

Arctic Circle lost by T.K.O.

Justice Scalia is here. Welcome, sir. May I be the first to say, you look fantastic. How are you?

Just talking some Sicilian with my *paisan*.

"Paisan" is Italian for "Partisan," right?

John McCain is here. John McCain, John McCain, what a maverick! Somebody find out what fork he used on his salad, because I guarantee you it wasn't a salad fork. This guy could have used a spoon! There's no predicting him. By the way, Senator McCain, it's so wonderful to see you coming back into the Republican fold. I have a summer house in South Carolina; look me up when

The "Straight-Talk Express" may, in fact, make local stops!!

Nagin will show you his righteous indignation for beads.

you go to speak at Bob Jones University. So glad you've seen the light, sir.

Mayor Nagin! Mayor Nagin is here from New Orleans, the chocolate city! Yeah, give it up. Mayor Nagin, I'd like to welcome you to Washington, D.C., the chocolate city with a marshmallow center. And a graham cracker crust of corruption. It's a Mallomar,[7] I guess is what I'm describing, a seasonal cookie.

Joe Wilson is here, Joe Wilson right down here in front, the most famous husband since Desi Arnaz. And of course he brought along his lovely wife Valerie Plame. Oh, my god. Oh, what have I said? I am sorry, Mr. President, I meant to say he brought along his lovely wife, Joe Wilson's wife. Patrick Fitzgerald is not here tonight? OK. Dodged a bullet.

And, of course, we can't forget the man of the hour, new press secretary, Tony Snow. Secret Service name, "Snow Job." Toughest job. What a hero. Took the second toughest job in government, next to, of course, the ambassador to Iraq.

Got some big shoes to fill, Tony. Big shoes to fill. Scott McClellan could say nothing like nobody else. McClellan, of course, eager to retire. Really felt like he needed to spend more time with Andrew Card's children. Mr. President, I wish you hadn't made the decision so quickly, sir.

I was vying for the job myself. I think I would have made a fabulous press secretary. I have nothing but contempt for these people. I know how to handle these clowns.

In fact, sir, I brought along an audition tape, and with your indulgence, I'd like to at least give it a shot. So, ladies and gentlemen, my press conference.

[*What followed was a riveting documentary on the dangers of Helen Thomas. Imagine that you are watching it.*]

Helen Thomas, ladies and gentlemen. Mr. Smith, members of the White House Correspondents' Association, Madame First Lady, Mr. President, it's been a true honor. Thank you very much. Good night!

★ ★ ★

---

[7] As desserts go, it's way better than the "Heckuva-Job" Brownie.

I'm happy to say my speech was met with respectful silence.[8] You could hear a pin drop. Or a sphincter clamp.

The President was the first one to greet me. "Well done," he said. That was payment enough. That, and the check in my breast pocket.

INDEX

ACKNOWLEDGMENTS

Without the support of the following groups and individuals, *I Am America (And So Can You)* would be merely *I Want to Be America (But How?)*

Thank you to Jamie Raab and her team at Grand Central Publishing; Bob Castillo, Jimmy Franco, Tom Whatley and Anne Twomey for their patience, counsel and trust.

Many thanks to Doyle Partners for their design prowess. Stephen Doyle, August Heffner, and Staci MacKenzie made this process a joyful collaboration.

Thanks to Jake Chessum and his crew for our beautiful cover and chapter photography.

Erica Myrickes was indispensable. And the book would not be possible without the enthusiasm, talent and support of Hilary Siegel, Katie Bruggeman, and the entire staff and crew of *The Colbert Report*.

Thanks to Robin Sanders for making this book legal.

Thank you to Jon Stewart for inspiration and guidance.

The photographic skills and intrepid spirits of John Bedolis and Andrew Matheson were essential, as were the wardrobe and make-up savvy of Antonia Xereas and Kerrie Plant-Price.

Thank you to Ben Karlin for his advice and encouragement.

Also, huge thanks to James Dixon, Dan Strone, Carrie Byalick, Cliff Gilbert-Lurie, Doug Herzog, Michele Ganeless and everyone at Comedy Central.

Finally, thanks to the following people who got us through this process and who we are lucky to have in our lives:

The Brumm Family and Camille March, Jennifer and Luka Buneta, The Community, Rita Cooley and the family, Leyla and Madison Dahm and the Dahm family, The Dinello Family and Your Soul Mate, The Dubbin family and Cailin Goldberg-Meehan, Christina Gausas, Glenn's family, Debra Downing Grosz, Emily Gwinn Hall, Adrian Jones, The Katsir/Schimer/Gold Family and Adina Lemeshow, The Krafft Family, The Lesser family, Sharon Long and the Long family, Anne Martin and Shermy, Meredith's family, The Silverman/Smart family, The McGee Family, Lorna Colbert and her Hilarious Brood, and Madeleine, Peter and John, and Evie McGee for her love and patience.

And to anyone we've forgotten, please accept our apologies, and we'll see you in the paperback.

ORIGINAL ILLUSTRATIONS AND GRAPHICS:
Andro Buneta
August Heffner
Kristopher Long
Amanda Pastenkos

ORIGINAL PHOTOGRAPHS:
John Bedolis
Jake Chessum
Andrew Matheson

PHOTOS/ ILLUSTRATIONS/ GRAPHICS:

COVER
Photography: **Jake Chessum;** Hair & Make-up Artist: **Kerri R. Plant-Price;** Wardrobe Stylist: **Antonia Xereas;** Digital Imaging: **Jonathan Podwil;** Illustration of Stephen (backcover flap): **Joe Quesada TM & © 2007 Marvel Characters, Inc. All Rights Reserved.**

INTRODUCTION
Chapter Opener: **Chessum.**

HOW TO READ
Sign: **Buneta.**

MY AMERICAN CHILDHOOD
Personal Photo: **Martin Luther Kindergarten.**

THE FAMILY
Chapter Opener: **Chessum;** Charles Manson: **AP;** Sly & the Family Stone **Getty Images;** Single Parent Family: **iStockphoto;** Old Maid: **Corbis;** Optical Illusion: **Buneta;** Grandparents: **iStockphoto;** Aunts and Uncles: **Corbis;** First Cousins: **iStockphoto;** Second Cousins: **AP;** 50th Cousins (planet earth): **iStockphoto.**

OLD PEOPLE
Chapter Opener: **Chessum;** Protein Pudding Coupon: **Buneta;** Elderly Maze (Funzone): **Long;** Oldest Man: **iStockphoto.**

ANIMALS
Chapter Opener: **Chessum;** Florida Cougar: **Getty Images;** California Condor: **Getty Images;** Hawaiian Monk Seal: **AP;** Ocelot: **Getty Images;** Pére David's Deer: **Getty Images;** Bighorn Sheep: **Getty Images;** Iberian Lynx: **Getty Images;**

Harry-Nosed Wombat: **iStockphoto;** Cow: **Mary Ann Kirigin;** Cow Diagram: **Buneta;** Food Pyramid: **Long;** Pat the Bunny: **Andrew Matheson;** FunZone Balls: Photos **John Bedolis/** Illustrations **Long.**

RELIGION
Chapter Opener: **Chessum;** Jesus: **Buneta;** Ozzy: **AP;** Gladys Knight & The Pips: **AP;** Crucifix: **Buneta;** Cross w/o Jesus: **Buneta;** Mormon Church: **iStockphoto;** Il David: **iStockphoto;** Hindu God: **iStockphoto;** Saint Sebastian: **Corbis;** Book inside Bible: **Matheson;** Travolta: **Photofest;** Matt Lauer: **AP;** Fat Joint: **Matheson;** Charles Darwin: **Library of Congress;** Waffles: **iStockphoto;** Ascent of God Illustration: **Buneta;** Burning Bush: **Long;** Fun Zone Religion Convert: **R. Dubbin.**

MY AMERICAN ADOLESCENCE
Personal Photo: **Porter-Gaud School.**

SPORTS
Chapter Opener: **Chessum;** Classic Smack: **Long;** World's Strongest Man: **Getty Images;** Advertise Here: **Buneta;** Kraft Seven Seas Dressing: **Matheson;** Caber Toss: **AP;** Sports Fan: **Matheson;** Nixon: **Library of Congress;** FDR: **Library of Congress;** T. Roosevelt: **Library of Congress;** Taft: **Library of Congress;** Liar's Poker: **Matheson;** Abstinence Bases: **Buneta.**

SEX & DATING
Chapter Opener: **Chessum;** Bandit with Sack: **Long;** Octopus: **iStockphoto;** Chimpanzee Sex: **Corbis;** Knight: **Buneta;** Damsel: **Long;** LeBron James: **Getty Images;** Dancing Feet: **Long;** Stephen Thumbs Up: **Chessum;** Soul Mate: **Buneta.**

HOMOSEXUAL AGENDA
Chapter Opener: **Chessum;** Men Kissing: **iStockphoto;** Throw Rug: **iStockphoto;** Clive Owen: **Getty Images;** Origami: **iStockphoto;** Dog Whisperer: **Getty Images;** Baby Carrots: **iStockphoto;** Mr. Sulu: **© 2007 CBS**

Studios Inc. STAR TREK and related marks are trademarks of CBS Studios Inc. All Rights Reserved; Neil Patrick Harris: **Corbis;** Formerly Gay Man: **Matheson;** Adopted child: **iStockphoto;** Gay Marriage: **Getty Images;** Tucked in T-Shirt: **Matheson;** Gay Clergy: **Getty Images;** Gay Leather Man: **Photo courtesy Hothouse.com;** Halloween Pug: **AP;** Oklahoma Cowboy: **iStockphoto;** Volley Ball: **iStockphoto;** Hannity Spots Colbert: **Long.**

HIGHER EDUCATION
Chapter Opener: **Chessum;** Ted Kaczynski: **AP;** Charlie Manson: **AP;** Gloria Steinman: **AP;** Evil Spock: **© 2007 CBS Studios Inc. STAR TREK and related marks are trademarks of CBS Studios Inc. All Rights Reserved;** Professor: **Matheson.**

HOLLYWOOD
Chapter Opener: **Chessum;** Morgan Freeman: **Photofest;** Groucho: **AP;** Gerbil: **iStockphoto;** Burl Ives: **Corbis;** E.Y. Harburg: **AP;** Bill Melendez: **Jeff Arnold;** Kim Hunter: **Corbis;** Larry Adler: **AP;** David Robison: **Paula Robison;** Judy Holiday: **Corbis;** George Clooney: **Photofest;** Sean Penn: **Getty Images;** Barbara Streisand: **Getty Images;** Tim Robbins: **Getty Images;** Kirsten Dunst: **Corbis;** Bring it On: **Photofest;** Marie Antoinette: **Photofest;** Leonardo Di Caprio: **Getty Images;** Rosie O'Donnell: **Getty Images;** Sheryl Crow: **Getty Images;** Alec Baldwin: **Corbis;** Mort Sinclair: **Getty Images;** Lion: **iStockphoto.**

MY AMERICAN MATURITY
Personal Photo: **Jim Margolis.**

THE MEDIA
Chapter Opener: **Chessum;** Katie Couric: **Getty Images;** Law & Order: **NBC/ Universal;** Charles Gibson: **ABC;** Wesley Snipes: **Corbis;** Car Bomb: **Getty Images;** Amy: **Corbis;** Tucker Carlson: **MSNBC;** James Carville: **Corbis;** Boston Cream Pie: **Matheson.**

CLASS
Chapter Opener: **Chessum;** Clerk: **Getty Images;** Rich Family: **Getty Images;** Poor Family: **Library of Congress;**

RACE
Chapter Opener: **Chessum;** The Invisible Man: **Photofest;** LBJ: **LBJ Library photo by Cecil Stoughton;** Race Track: **Long;** Ex-Civil Rights Leader: **Matheson.**

IMMIGRATION
Chapter Opener: **Chessum;** Berlin Wall: **AP;** Pottery Mug: **iStockphoto;** Old Colossus: **Paul Smith TM & ©2007 Marvel Characters, Inc. All Rights Reserved;** Ocupado Plaque: **Long;** Sports Fan: **Matheson.**

SCIENCE
Chapter Opener: **Buneta;** Atronomy Triangulum: **Long;** DNA Illustration: **iStockphoto;** USA vs. Periodic Table: **Long;** Prof. Wonder: **Mark Wenzel;** Fishbowl: **Long;** Pitcher of Water: **iStockphoto;** Hamster: **iStockphoto;**

A NOTE TO THE FUTURE
Chapter Opener: **Chessum.**

WHAT HAVE WE LEARNED
Chapter Opener: **Chessum.**

HOW TO RETIRE THIS BOOK
Instruction Illustrations: **Buneta.**

WHITE HOUSE CORRESPONDENTS DINNER
WH Illustration: **Corbis;** Pages 220-225: **White House Correspondents' Association;** Page 227: **Getty Images.**